Cambridge Marketing Handbook
Law

Cambridge Marketing Handbook
Law

Marketing Communications and the Law

Kiran Kapur

Publisher's note

Every possible effort has been made to ensure that the information contained in this book is accurate at the time of going to press, and the publishers and authors cannot accept responsibility for any errors or omissions, however caused. No responsibility for loss or damage occasioned to any person acting, or refraining from action, as a result of the material in this publication can be accepted by the editor, the publisher or any of the authors.

First published in Great Britain and the United States in 2013 by Kogan Page Limited in association with Cambridge Marketing Press.

Apart from any fair dealing for the purposes of research or private study, or criticism or review, as permitted under the Copyright, Designs and Patents Act 1988, this publication may only be reproduced, stored or transmitted, in any form or by any means, with the prior permission in writing of the publishers, or in the case of reprographic reproduction in accordance with the terms and licences issued by the CLA. Enquiries concerning reproduction outside these terms should be sent to the publishers at the undermentioned addresses:

120 Pentonville Road	1518 Walnut Street,	4737/23 Ansari Road
London N1 9JN	Suite 1100	Daryaganj
United Kingdom	Philadelphia PA 19102	New Delhi 110002
	USA	India

www.koganpage.com

© 2013, Cambridge Marketing College.
Edited and proofread by Melissa Nixon and Emma Garland. Diagrams and charts redrawn by Graham Berridge.

The right of Cambridge Marketing College to be identified as the author of this work has been asserted by them in accordance with the Copyright, Designs and Patents Act 1988.

ISBN   978 0 7494 7067 8
British Library Cataloguing-in-Publication Data

A CIP record for this book is available from the British Library.

Design and layout by Cambridge Marketing College
Printed and bound by CPI/Antony Rowe, Chippenham, Wiltshire.

Dedication
To my parents for their unending support and encouragement.

About the author

Kiran has worked predominately in Financial Services and has expertise in customer relationship marketing and customer communications. As a consultant, she has worked as project manager for companies including Liverpool Victoria, Barclays, London Life and Cazenove.

She has taught a wide variety of courses at Cambridge Marketing College since 1999. She is the Distance Learning & Overseas Course Director, with responsibility for the College's overseas expansion and a Fellow of the College. She has been a CIM examiner since 2004. Her publications include the Assessing the Marketing Environment Study Guide published by Pearson Education in 2009. She is a trustee of Jimmy's Cambridge, a charity for homeless people.

Disclaimer
This Handbook is not legal advice and is not a substitute for legal advice. You should obtain competent legal advice on anything discussed in this Handbook and not rely upon the explanations of the legal guidance set out in this Handbook. These materials are intended solely to help you determine when to seek professional advice. While every effort has been made to make these materials as accurate as possible, the matters discussed here are complex and these materials are necessarily simplistic and incomplete. The author will not be responsible for any errors.

We are grateful to the specialist ad law team at Osborne Clarke for their permission to adapt certain content from their website www.marketinglaw.co.uk. However the content of this book is the responsibility of the author and is not endorsed or approved by Osborne Clarke, whose views it does not necessarily represent.

Cambridge Marketing Handbook: Law by Kiran Kapur

Contents

Word Cloud	7
Preface	8
Introduction	9

Chapter 1: CPR and BPR — 12
1.1 Consumer Protection from Unfair Trading Regulations 2008 (CPR) — 12
1.2 The Business Protection from Misleading Marketing Regulations 2008 (BPR) — 16

Chapter 2: The CAP Code — 22
2.1 General rules — 25
2.2 Making marketing communications clear – CAP Code Section 2 — 26
2.3 Misleading claims – CAP Code Section 3 — 27
2.4 Pricing – CAP Code Section 3 — 29
2.5 Availability – CAP Code Section 3 — 34
2.6 Comparisons – CAP Code Section 3 — 34
2.7 Endorsements and testimonials – CAP Code Section 3 — 35
2.8 Guarantee/warranty/after-sales service/care packages – CAP Code Section 3 — 35
2.9 Offence – CAP Code Section 3 — 36
2.10 Marketing alcohol – CAP Code Section 18 — 38
2.11 Marketing to children – CAP Code Section 5 — 38
2.12 Privacy – CAP Code Section 6 — 42
2.13 Sales promotions – CAP Code Section 8 — 43
2.14 Distance selling – CAP Code Section 9 — 45
2.15 Data protection – CAP Code section 10 — 45
2.16 Political advertisements – CAP Code Section 7 — 46
2.17 Other CAP rules for specialised areas — 46

Chapter 3: Distance Selling — 47

Chapter 4: Product Placement (Ofcom Broadcasting Code) — 55

Chapter 5: Provision of Services Regulations 2009 (PSR) — 58

Chapter 6: Data Protection — 65
6.1 Data Protection Act 1998 — 65
6.2 The Privacy and Electronic Communications Regulations (PECR) — 68
6.3 E-mail marketing – legal requirements — 73
6.4 Telemarketing and fax marketing — 75
6.5 Direct marketing — 76
6.6 Cookie law — 77
6.7 Viral marketing — 80
6.8 Public electronic communications service providers — 81

Chapter 7: Premium Rate Telephone Services (PRS) — 82

Chapter 8: UK Code of Broadcast Advertising (BCAP) — 85
8.1 General rules – BCAP Code Sections 01 and 02 — 86
8.2 Making advertising clear – BCAP Code Section 03 — 89
8.3 Pricing – BCAP Code Section 03 — 89
8.4 Availability – BCAP Code Section 03 — 92
8.5 Comparisons – BCAP Code Section 03 — 93
8.6 Endorsements and testimonials – BCAP Code Section 03 — 94
8.7 Guarantee/Warranty/After-sales service/Care packages – BCAP Code Section 03 — 94
8.8 Offence – BCAP – Code Section 04 — 95
8.9 Children – BCAP – Code Section 05 — 97
8.10 Privacy – BCAP –Code Section 08 — 104
8.11 Political advertisements – BCAP Code Section 07 — 105
8.12 Other BCAP rules for specialised areas — 106

Further Reading — 107
Index — 109

Cambridge Marketing Handbook: Law by Kiran Kapur

Word clouds produced through Wordle™ (www.wordle.net)

Preface

This is not a book about marketing legal services. This book is designed to help you with the legal issues that marketers need to be aware of in the course of their work. A caveat – I am a marketer not a lawyer, so my view is practical not legal (I think that is a good thing!). Legal language is very precise, but uses words not used in normal life. As far as possible, I have aimed to use colloquial language for clarity but do note this means some of the legal niceties and nuance will have been removed.

If you have a specific legal problem, you should consult a lawyer – you have free access to one if you are a member of the Chartered Institute of Marketing, and other professional bodies.

This book looks at English Law, covering England and Wales. Scotland has its own legal jurisdiction and, whilst some aspects of English Law will apply, others will not.

As a marketer, these are the issues I come up against when I want to understand the legal issues:

- advertising – print (Chapter 2), broadcast (Chapter 8)
- cookie law (Chapter 3)
- social media (Chapter 2)
- distance selling (Chapter 3)
- promotions and incentives (Chapter 2)
- data protection (Chapter 6)
- selling to children (Chapters 2 and 8)
- consumer protection legislation – CPR and BPR (Chapter 1)

Each chapter contains:

- a brief overview of the rules and regulations
- more details on the rules
- examples of good and/or bad practice
- check lists

Introduction

Marketing is subject to both legislation in the form of Acts of Parliament and self-regulation.

Legislation

Many new laws have come into effect since 2006, including the Consumer Protection from Unfair Trading Regulations 2008, Business Protection from Misleading Marketing Regulations 2008 and the Amendment to the Privacy and Electronic Communications Regulations 2011, otherwise known as the 'cookie law'. Two important pieces of regulation are the Consumer Protection from Unfair Trading Regulations 2008 (CPR) and the Business Protection from Misleading Marketing Regulations 2008 (BPR).

Self-regulation

This is the traditional form of regulation for marketing. One of the main upholders of this regulation is the Advertising Standards Authority (ASA) which enforces the CAP Code of Conduct. Other industry bodies charged with enforcing self-regulation are the Financial Services Authority (FSA), Office of Fair Trading (OFT) and Trading Standards Services (TSS).

I have taken the view in this book that most marketers are not interested in the penalties of not obeying the rules, or whether the rules are by Law or self-regulation. Most marketers just want to comply with the rules and get on with the job.

Where do I start?

The biggest problem is deciding which areas of legislation affect your organisation. The table overleaf summarises the key legislation/regulation. The 'Does it affect me?' section in each chapter will also help you.

Marketing business/issue	Relevant legislation/regulations	Where to look
B2C	Consumer Protection from Unfair Trading Regulations 2008 (CPR)	Chapter 1.1
	The CAP Code	Chapter 2
	The BCAP Code	Chapter 8
	Business Protection from Misleading Marketing Regulations 2008 (BPR) (if comparative advertising)	Chapter 1.2
	Data Protection Act 1998	Chapter 6.1
	Privacy & Electronic Communications Regulations (PECR)	Chapter 6.2
	Distance Selling Regulations (DSR) and Electronic Commerce (EC Directive) Regulations 2002 (ECR)	Chapter 3
	Provision of Services Regulations 2009 (PSR)	Chapter 5
B2B	BPR	Chapter 1.2
	CPR (if products are sold on to consumers)	Chapter 1.1
	The CAP Code	Chapter 2
	The BCAP Code	Chapter 8
	Data Protection Act 1988	Chapter 6.1
	Privacy & Electronic Communications Regulations (PECR)	Chapter 6.2
	Provision of Services Regulations 2009 (PSR)	Chapter 5
Advertising	The CAP Code	Chapter 2
	The BCAP Code	Chapter 8
Comparative Advertising	BPR	Chapter 1.2
	The CAP Code	Chapter 2.6
	The BCAP Code	Chapter 8
Direct Marketing	DM Code of Practice	Chapter 3
	Privacy & Electronic Communications Regulations (PECR)	Chapter 6.5
Distance/Online Selling	DM Code of Practice	Chapter 3
	The BCAP Code	Chapter 8
	DSR & ECR	Chapter 3
	Data Protection Act 1998	Chapter 6.1

Email Marketing	Privacy & Electronic Communications Regulations (PECR)	Chapter 6.3
	The CAP Code	
	ECR	Chapter 3
Marketing to Children	CAP Code Section 5	Chapter 2.11
	The BCAP Code	Chapter 8.9
Personal Information	Data Protection Act 1988	Chapter 6.1
	PECR (including The Cookie Law)	Chapter 6.2
	CAP Code Section 10	
Premium Rate Telephone Services	PhonepayPlus Code of Practice	Chapter 7
Product Placement	OfCom Broadcasting Code	Chapter 4
Services Marketing	Provision of Services Regulations 2009 (PSR)	Chapter 5
Sales Promotion	CAP Code Section 8	Chapter 2.13
Viral Marketing	PECR	Chapter 6.7

Chapter 1: CPR and BPR
1.1 Consumer Protection from Unfair Trading Regulations 2008 (CPR)

Overview
Consumer Protection Regulations and their counterpart the BPR (Business Protection Legislation) have been introduced to harmonise EU laws. This removes the previous danger of running campaigns that are legal in one EU country but not in another.

Compliance with CPR will, for most businesses, simply be a part of good business practice. The rules outlaw what is clearly poor practice – such as door stepping customers or lying about your products. The rules are specific but there is a general 'catch-all' statement that unfair commercial practices are prohibited[1].

The Protection is designed to help an average consumer make a free and informed purchasing decision.

Does it affect me?
The Protection mainly refers to B2C marketing, but might affect B2B if your products are sold on to consumers. For example, a business supplying food to a supermarket would need to ensure its labelling is compliant.

---

1 **Sources:** Information in this section was taken from www.marketinglaw.co.uk, http://www.out-law.com/page9050; http://www.oft.gov.uk/business-advice/treating-customers-fairly/protection;

How does it work?

1. Practices are anything that relate to the sale or supply of a product/service: before, after and during the sale, and any cancellation.
2. There are 31 practices that are forbidden outright.
3. Other actions may be classified as unfair practices. Unfair practices are classified as misleading actions, misleading omissions and aggressive practices. Practices are unfair if they would cause a consumer to carry out an action they would otherwise not have done. The action does not have to be to make a purchase, it could be to enter a premises.

Forbidden practices

There are 31 practices that are forbidden altogether. These are obviously poor practice, so compliance should not cause problems for most businesses. The banned practices include:

- misuse of a trust or quality mark by falsely claiming a trader has a qualification or award or is a member of a professional body
- saying something is free when it is not
- persistent cold-calling or emailing
- falsely claiming someone has won a prize
- falsely claiming that something the consumer is entitled to in law is a distinctive benefit of the product
- false 'closing down' sales
- ignoring requests to leave someone's home
- claiming that a failure to purchase will jeopardise the trader's livelihood
- masquerading as a consumer, such as writing advertorials or reviews about your product/company whilst pretending to be a customer
- using scare tactics to give the consumer the impression their safety will be jeopardised without the product
- directly exhorting children to buy a product or persuade an adult to buy the product for them

A complete list of the 31 banned practices, with examples, can be found at www.oft.gov.uk/shared_oft/business_leaflets/cpregs/oft1008.pdf.

Unfair practices
These are divided into misleading actions, misleading omissions and aggressive practices. Misleading actions include making false or misleading claims.

An example would be marketing a product in a way that creates confusion with a competitor's product (such as using a similar brand name or logo). Another example would be falsely telling a consumer that a boiler needs replacing when it could be repaired.

Misleading omissions include hiding information about a product/service or providing incomplete or untimely information. An example would be not telling a consumer that a contract must run for a minimum period, or not giving full details of the price of a product/service. Aggressive practices include harassment, coercion or undue influence.

To be deemed unfair, the practice is likely to prevent the average consumer from making an informed decision. In other words, by undertaking this unfair practice, the business has enticed the consumer to make a purchase, or enter a shop or cancel a product.

Average consumer
There is an assumption that your practices are aimed at an average consumer – the traditional idea of 'the man in the street' or 'the man on the Clapham omnibus'. However, your target consumer should also be considered. So if your target consumers are a disability group, the practices would be considered unfair if they were likely to prevent an average person from that disability group from making an informed choice.

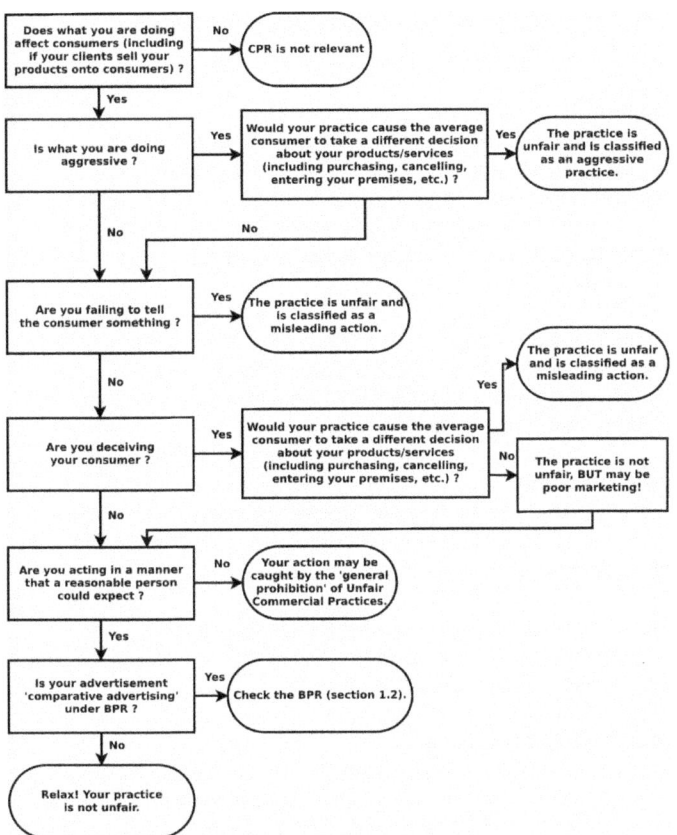

Figure 1.1 Are you in breach of the CPR?[2]

---

[2] **Sources:** adapted from http://www.oft.gov.uk/shared_oft/business_leaflets/cpregs/oft1008.pdf

1.2 The Business Protection from Misleading Marketing Regulations 2008[3] (BPR)

Overview
B2B advertising: the BPRs ban misleading business-to-business advertising. 'Advertising' has a wide definition and includes all promotions about a product/service in a commercial context, including traditional advertising, oral statements, catalogues, on-line advertising and packaging. Compliance is likely to be standard practice for most B2B marketers.

Comparative advertising: any comparisons in B2C or B2B contexts are regulated by the BPRs. Comparative advertising is advertising that identifies a competitor or a product of a competitor. This is the more complicated part of the legislation.

Does it affect me?
It affects you if you advertise in any way your goods/services to other businesses. But compliance is not difficult, and you are likely to find your normal practices are sufficient.

The comparative advertising regulations affect you if your advertisements identify a competitor or a competitor's product. This applies to both B2B and B2C advertisements.

Misleading B2B advertising
Advertising is defined broadly to mean "any form of representation which is made in connection with a trade, business, craft or profession in order to promote the supply or transfer of a product".

---

3 **Sources:** http://www.oft.gov.uk/business-advice/treating-customers-fairly/advertising/business-protection, http://www2.eastriding.gov.uk/business/trading-standards/fair-trading/a-guide-to-the-business-protection-from-misleading-marketing-regulations/, http://www.oft.gov.uk/shared_oft/business_leaflets/general/oft1056.pdf, http://www.royds.com/wp-content/uploads/2009/05/The-business-protection-marketing-regulations-2008.pdf, http://www.olswang.com/pdfs/mmr_may08.pdf

It includes face-to-face oral statements, telemarketing, descriptions accompanying goods (including claims on packaging), as well as advertising in the traditional sense of the word.

An advertisement is misleading if:

- it deceives, or is likely to deceive the traders it addresses or reaches, and
- the deception is likely to affect the economic behaviour of those traders, or
- as a result of the above effect on traders it injures or is likely to injure a competitor in some way.

An advertisement can be deceptive if it:

- contains a false statement of fact;
- conceals or leaves out important facts;
- promises to do something but there is no intention of carrying it out;
- creates a false impression, even if everything stated in it may be literally true.

In other words, if you lie in your advertisement or only tell part of the truth, then you are misleading the trader. If your deception makes the trader take a decision they would not otherwise have taken, then you have broken the law.

Comparative advertising

Comparative advertising identifies a competitor or a product of a competitor. In order to be allowed, it has to meet all the conditions in the BPRs.

This is a complicated part of the legislation and it is giving rise to case law as companies are taking each other to court. The easiest way to comply is to be scrupulously careful over any comparisons that you make.

For example, an advertisement says "x% preferred our drink to a leading cola drink". This is a comparative advertisement because, although the leading cola drink is not named, it could be clearly assumed that there is one leading cola drink. If an advertisement stated the interest paid on a savings account was higher than another's, then the comparison should be between two identical accounts, or the differences made clear. So the advertising bank could not claim it had better interest rates if it was comparing its two year account with a rival's instant access account.

An easier mistake to make would be if your company's sales person says something about a competitor to a potential customer: "Their prices are cheaper because Company X uses inexperienced installers". This is denigrating Company X and is against the law.

You must also not confuse a customer over whether your company is the same as a well-known company. Naming a product so that it appears to be a competitor's (such as claiming you sell ipads when your product is not an Apple product) is illegal.

Your comparative advertising must:

- provide objective comparisons of products on a like-for-like basis;
- not discredit or denigrate a competitor or its brand;
- not take unfair advantage of the reputation of a competitor's brand; and
- not create confusion between your company and a competitor, or its brands.

Comparative advertising is allowed if the advertisement:

- is not misleading under the BPRs or the CPRs
- compares products that meet the same needs or are intended for the same purpose
- objectively compares one or more material, relevant, verifiable and representative feature(s) of those products. This may include price
- does not create confusion, either between the advertiser and a competitor, or between trade marks (or similar) of products of the advertiser and those of a competitor
- does not discredit, denigrate or take unfair advantage of a competitor's trade mark (or similar)
- for products with designation of origin relates in each case to products with the same designation
- does not take unfair advantage of the reputation of a trade mark (or similar) of a competitor or of the designation of origin of competing products
- does not present products as imitations or replicas of products bearing a protected trade mark or trade name

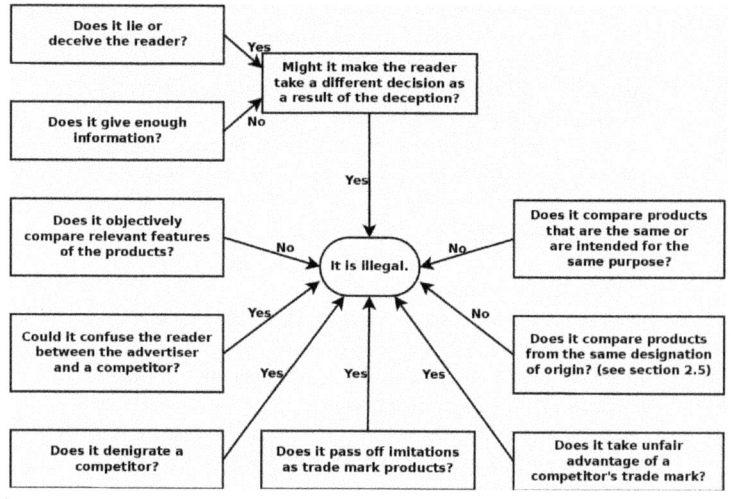

Figure 1.2 Is your comparative advertisement misleading?[4]

---

[4] **Source:** taken from http://www.oft.gov.uk/shared_oft/business_leaflets/general/oft1056.pdf

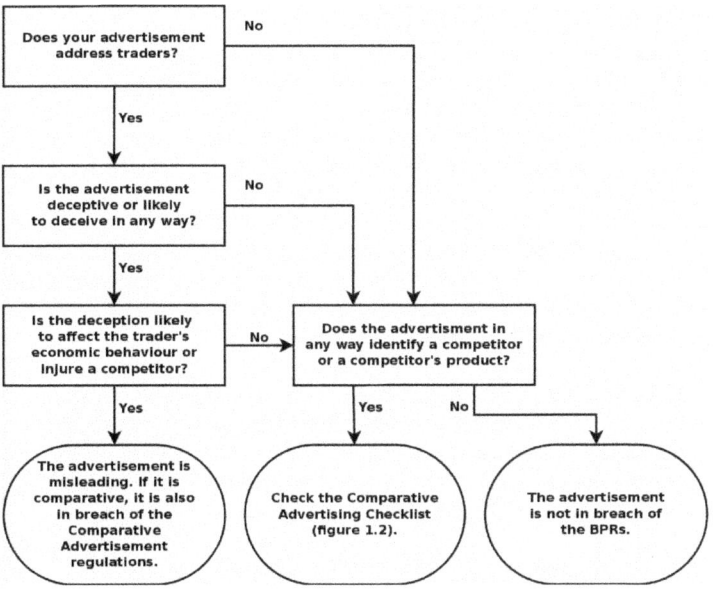

Figure 1.3 Is your B2B advertising misleading?[5]

---

5 **Source:** http://www.oft.gov.uk/shared_oft/business_leaflets/general/oft1056flow.pdf

Chapter 2: The CAP Code

The Committee of Advertising Practice (CAP) covers non-broadcast advertising. There is a BCAP Code (Broadcast Committee of Advertising Practice) – see Chapter 8. The CAP Code and its twin, the Broadcast Code of Advertising Practice (BCAP) were brought into line in 2010 and now closely mirror each other, making the regulation a lot less confusing.

In the UK, The UK Code of Non-broadcast Advertising, Sales Promotion and Direct Marketing (The CAP code) is the rule book for non-broadcast advertisements, sales promotions and direct marketing communications[6].

Essentially, the Code is designed to ensure marketing communications are legal, decent, honest and truthful. Most importantly for marketers, the Code is enforced in the spirit as well as the letter. In other words, it is a not a defence to say "but the Code doesn't specifically stop me" if your communication breaks the spirit of the Code.

The Codes are written by the Committees and enforced by the ASA. The ASA is funded by the advertising industry, through a levy on advertising space and direct mail. The ASA can apply a variety of sanctions such as insisting all advertisements are removed or by insisting on future pre-vetting of all advertisements.

The CAP code was rewritten in 2010 but there are updates issued by the ASA. This guide covers the amendments made to beginning May 2013. To check for additional updates, go to http://www.cap.org.uk/Advertising-Codes.aspx.

The CAP code applies to nearly any form of marketing you are likely to consider doing, plus a few things you might not think of. So it logically applies to printed advertisements, posters, catalogues and direct mail.

---

[6] **Source:** Preface of the non-broadcast CAP code

But it also applies to SMS marketing, marketing databases, and on-line advertising, including paid for search engine listing.

Does it affect me?
The CAP code covers all marketing communications (see box for the full list). Basically, if you do any form of marketing communications, including marketing messages on your website, Facebook or Twitter, then it applies to you.

The CAP code includes provisions from the CPR and BPR. This Chapter considers the additional areas of the Code. So start by reading the CPR and BPR Chapter.

The complete list of non-broadcast media covered by the CAP Code is:

1. advertisements in newspapers, magazines, brochures, leaflets, circulars, mailings, e-mails, text transmissions (including SMS and MMS), fax transmissions, catalogues, follow-up literature and other electronic or printed material;
2. posters and other promotional media in public places, including moving images;
3. cinema, video, DVD and Blu-ray advertisements;
4. advertisements in non-broadcast electronic media, including but not limited to: online advertisements in paid-for space (including banner or pop-up advertisements and online video advertisements); paid-for search listings; preferential listings on price comparison sites; viral advertisements; in-game advertisements; commercial classified advertisements; advergames that feature in display advertisements; advertisements transmitted by Bluetooth; advertisements distributed through web widgets and online sales promotions and prize promotions;
5. marketing databases containing consumers' personal information;
6. sales promotions in non-broadcast media;
7. advertorials;
8. advertisements and other marketing communications by or from companies, organisations or sole traders on their own websites, or in other non-paid-for space online under their control, that are directly connected with the supply or transfer of goods, services, opportunities and gifts, or which consist of direct solicitations of donations as part of their own fund-raising activities.

Note: If you are promotiong premium-rate telephone services, you must abide by both the CAP Code and PhonepayPlus regulation (see Chapter 7).

What does the code not apply to?
Broadcast advertisements – see the BCAP Code in Chapter 8.

It does not apply to:

- Advertisements in foreign media: if the communication originates from outside the UK or is on non-UK websites but targeted at UK consumers, then it comes under the jurisdiction of the country of origin
- Claims addressed purely to professionals: medical, dental or veterinary practitioners
- Classified private ads, both on and off-line
- Statutory public information, including official notices
- Private correspondence, including customer service correspondence
- Press releases
- Editorial content, including website editorial
- Regular crosswords
- Packaging, wrappers, labels, tickets, timetables and price lists, unless they include advertising
- Point of sale displays – but see Sales Promotions (section 2.13)

However, as a marketer, what you want to know is "is my piece of communication compliant?" So let's consider each element in turn. If you need advice on an advertisement, the CAP has a copy advice team who offer advice free of charge. The team will look at ideas, concepts, imagery and copy for your advertisements and claim to offer fast and confidential advice. Contact http://www.cap.org.uk/Advice-Training-on-the-rules/Bespoke-Copy-Advice.aspx.

2.1 General rules
Marketers should deal fairly with consumers.

Marketing communications must comply with the law and not encourage anyone to break it.

Marketing communications must be easily identifiable as a marketing communication. You cannot hide a piece of marketing as an editorial.

Advertorials must be clearly labelled for example by labelling as an 'advertisement feature'. An advertorial is an advertisement in the form of an editorial.

One area where this can cause problems is Twitter. Celebrities paid to support your product and sending out Twitter messages about it must make this clear, for example by using #ad (see Twitter section below). The commercial intent must be obvious.

> **Toni & Guy Hairdressers**
>
> **July 2012**
> Actress Gemma Collins tweeted about a Toni & Guy hairdressers suggesting a particular branch was good and offering a 10% discount. #ad was not used. The ASA investigated and said that this broke the rules.

2.2 Making marketing communications clear – CAP Code Section 2

It must be clear that a marketing communication is a piece of marketing.

Email
Unsolicited e-mail marketing must be identifiable as marketing communications without having to open them.

Twitter
Tweets that are commercially driven, or written by someone paid to support the company, must be clearly identified as advertising.

The ASA consider that the average Twitter user follows a number of people on the site and that they would receive a number of tweets throughout the day, which they might scroll through quickly. So Twitter 'ads' must be obviously identifiable as marketing communications.

Mars Chocolate UK Ltd

March 2012
Mars arranged a twitter campaign of 5 tweets from Rio Ferdinand sent within one hour. These tweets were:

- "Really getting into the knitting!!! Helps me relax after high-pressure world of the Premiership"
- "Can't wait 2 get home from training and finish that cardigan"
- "Just popping out 2 get more wool!!!"
- "Cardy finished. Now 4 the matching mittens!!!"
- "You're not you when you're hungry @snickersUk#hungry#spon ..." The final tweet included a picture of Rio Ferdinand holding a Snickers bar.

The ASA agreed this did meet the CAP code because the 5 tweets were sent out in the space of an hour, and the first 4 did not mention a product. Only the last tweet showed a product – a Snickers bar – and this was clearly identifiable as a marketing communication.

2.3 Misleading claims – CAP Code Section 3
Marketing communications must not mislead. You can include puffery ('exaggerated claims' that the average consumer is unlikely to take literally) provided you are not deliberately misleading.

You cannot pass off expressions of opinion as an objective claim. You cannot claim that something is universally accepted if there is a significant disagreement about it, such as a differing scientific opinion. If you make a claim, you must be able to substantiate it.

> **Weston Knightly Ltd trading as British Gold Refinery**
>
> **January 2012**
> A Google sponsored search ad stated "Scrap Gold We Pay 70% More For Scrap Gold. Go Direct, Cut Out the Middleman".
>
> When challenged by the ASA, the company could not find any evidence to substantiate this 70% more claim, so the ASA ruled the ad could not be run again.

Marketing communications must not mislead by giving unclear, unintelligible, ambiguous or untimely information. Marketing Communications must not hide material information. Material information is the information the consumer needs to make an informed decision on the product/service. If there is not space to give the material information, then it must be clear where this information is available.

You may not promote a pyramid promotion scheme (sometimes called Ponzi schemes) where consumers pay for the opportunity to receive payments primarily from other new members, not the sale or consumption of products.

If you are quoting prices in your communications, material information is:

- the main characteristics of the product;
- the identity (for example, a trading name) and geographical address of the marketer and any other trader on whose behalf the marketer is acting;
- the price of the advertised product, including taxes. If the price cannot be calculated in advance, then how the price will be calculated;
- delivery charges;

- the arrangements for payment, delivery, performance or complaint handling. You only have to explain these if your arrangements are not what a consumer would normally expect;
- if consumers have the right to withdraw or cancel.

2.4 Pricing – CAP Code Section 3

Essentially, if you quote a price, it must be the price the consumer must pay. This includes any non-optional duties, fees and taxes, plus any delivery charges. If any of these costs are variable, then you must explain how the costs are calculated.

If prices are shown VAT-free, then the VAT rates that some consumers will have to pay must be prominently stated.

If the price of one product depends on buying another one (such as "buy product x, get product y half price"), then it must be clear what the consumer must pay or do to get the advertised price.

Price comparison[7]

You must be very clear about the basis of a price comparison for your price against a competitor. You will need to have evidence that justifies your claim. Any significant conditions attached to price promises should be stated.

---

7 **Source:** CAP Helpnote: Lowest price claims and price promises, updated February 2013
http://www.cap.org.uk/Advice-Training-on-the-rules/Help-Notes/Lowest-Price-Claims-and-Promises.aspx

Definitions:

lowest prices	means you will beat competitors' prices, you have monitored the competitors' prices
best prices	means you will beat competitors' prices, you have monitored the competitors' prices
price promise	for example, to beat a competitor's lower price if informed of that price by a consumer. Not necessarily the same as a 'lowest price' claim
lowest prices guaranteed	is a price promise and means the product cannot be bought as cheaply or cheaper elsewhere. The claim must be verifiable
lowest prices guarantee	is a price claim
price match	matching, not beating, a competitor's price for example: 'no one beats our prices', 'unbeatable low prices', 'we won't be beaten on price' or 'unbeatable price guarantee'

Claims that you charge the 'lowest price' or 'best price' mean that you will always beat, not just match, competitors' prices. If you mean this only to apply to a sample of products, then you must specify that sample clearly, for example by explaining that it is based on a typical weekly shop and stating where consumers can find information about the products compared. You will need to be able to demonstrate that it is a fair and suitable basis for a general savings claim.

If the claim is based on prices for a selection of products, you should give a list of the selected products either in the ad or in material that consumers can easily locate.

If a 'lowest price' claim is based on monitoring carried out on a specific date, the marketing communication should include that date. The monitoring should be carried out as close as possible to the appearance or distribution date of the advertisement.

A 'price promise' (for example, to beat a competitor's lower price if informed of that price by a consumer) does not necessarily justify a 'lowest price' claim, unless it is backed up with monitoring of the competitors' products.

Marketers offering to match, but not beat, competitors' prices should ensure that their ad reflects that clearly.

Marketers should ensure that 'lowest price' claims either in media with long copy deadlines (for example, magazines) or with a long shelf-life (for example, directories or brochures) are accurate when the ad appears and remain so for the duration of its appearance.

'Unbeatable low prices' claims and promises
Marketers that offer to match but not beat competitors' prices, or that offer a price promise to match but not beat competitors' lowest prices, should ensure that they do not imply that they will beat competitors' prices. They could, for example, claim 'no one beats our prices', 'unbeatable low prices', 'we won't be beaten on price' or 'unbeatable price guarantee'. Marketers must be able to support those claims.

'Free/Gratis/Without Charge'
'Free' means free! Do not describe something as free and then make the consumer pay. You must be clear what the consumer has to do to get the free offer.

A product is not 'free':

- if the consumer has to pay other charges to get it – such as postage, packaging, handling or administration costs
- where the consumer has to buy a product to get another one free:
    - you cannot increase the price of the product that has to be bought to cover the cost of the promotion
    - you cannot reduce the quality of the product that the consumer must buy

'Free trial' must not be used to describe 'satisfaction or your money back' offers, because the consumer has to pay for the product to try it.

CAP and BCAP give examples of using the word 'free'[8]:

✓ "free wallchart when you buy Thursday's paper" is justified if the paper is sold without a wallchart on other days for the same price;

✓ "25% extra free", for a bottle of shampoo, is justified if the bottle contains 25% more shampoo than is usually supplied at that price;

✓ "free travel insurance for customers who book their holiday online" is justified if customers who book the same journey by telephone are offered the same price but not offered free insurance, or if internet customers who choose to buy their insurance from a different provider pay the same for their holiday as those who choose to take advantage of the marketer's insurance offer;

✓ "free delivery for customers who spend over £50 on groceries" is justified if the retailer does not offer free delivery when the grocery spend is less than £50.

In each case, the company can demonstrate that there is a genuinely separate element that is 'free'. If the customer does not comply with the rules of the offer, they do not receive the free addition.

Slightly more confusing is the use of the word 'free' in part of a package of products. For example, if a mobile phone subscription offers a certain amount of airtime, texts and voicemail, this is described as a package. Customers cannot choose to have only part of this package, so the marketer cannot claim that it is 'free'.

---

8 **Source:** Guidance Note: Guidance on the use of the 'free', published by CAP (Sept 2010)

If a new element is introduced, such as picture texts, at no additional cost, then the marketer may claim this is 'free' but only for a short time (usually up to 6 months). After 6 months, the customer will assume this is part of the package, and no longer a free benefit.

Introductory offers: Existing products to potential new customers[9]
Similar rules apply to using 'free':

✓ 'Free sports bag for new members' of a gym would be justified if the sports bag was offered to all new members, who could choose whether or not to take it, and new members paid the same price whether or not they took the bag.

✓ 'Free calls for the first three months' could be justified, even on an ongoing basis where the paid-for item is a package. You would need to show that the offer was open only to new customers and that existing customers who paid the same price did not receive inclusive calls but received an otherwise identical service: you would have demonstrated that the calls were more than was usually supplied for the price and so justified the use of 'free'.

New product
As the product is new, the marketer cannot show that there has been a product at the same price before. To justify the use of 'free', the marketer must show that the customer has a genuine choice over whether to have the free item or not. For example, if a new magazine is launched with the offer 'Free binder with issue one' with a genuine choice of whether the customer took the binder, the marketer would have shown that the offer was a conditional-purchase promotion and justified the use of 'free'.

---

9 **Source:** Guidance on the use of the "free", published by CAP (Sept 2010)

2.5 Availability – CAP Code Section 3
If you advertise a product, it must be available.

If demand is likely to exceed supply, you must be clear that this is a limited offer. Once stocks run out, you must stop running the marketing communication.

If the offer is just testing the amount of potential demand, you must state this clearly.

Any restrictions on availability, such as geographic or age restrictions, must be clear.

You cannot refuse to take an order for the product, or refuse to deliver it in a reasonable time frame, in an attempt to sell another one (this is called 'switch selling').

You cannot mislead the consumer about the possibility of finding a product elsewhere to encourage the consumer to buy the product on less favourable conditions.

2.6 Comparisons – CAP Code Section 3
This is an area of potential confusion.

Claims that your product is superior ('superlative claims') will be assumed to be against all competing products. Claims that your product is superior must be supported by evidence. The only time you do not need to have evidence is if your claims are 'puffery', that is something the consumer is unlikely to take literally. If you claim your product is superior, you must be clear exactly what is superior.

Comparison with an identifiable competitor: the general advice is to be very careful here. You must compare products that are intended for the same purpose, you must make claims that are clear, relevant and verifiable. You must not cause confusion with the competitor.

EU agricultural products and foods: if these have a 'designation of origin' then you must compare only with other products with the same designation.

Price comparisons: the rule is to compare like with like. If you are comparing your price against your competitors, it must be for the same product!

2.7 Endorsements and testimonials – CAP Code Section 3

Put simply, keep a record and be clear what the testimonial is about – if it is for Product X, do not claim it is for something different.

If you quote an endorsement or testimonial, you must be able to show that it is genuine and keep a copy of it. You must also get permission to use it. You do not need permission to make an accurate quote from a published source, test, trial, professional endorsement, research facility or professional journal.

Endorsements that are obviously fictitious may be used.

Never use Royal Arms or Emblems or Royal Warrant without prior permission. Never imply you are endorsed by the ASA or CAP.

2.8 Guarantee/warranty/after-sales service/care packages – CAP Code Section 3

If you offer a guarantee, you must abide by it. Be very clear about any restrictions.

If the consumer claims a refund under the guarantee, you must refund promptly.

If you are offering products in European Economic Area (EEA) states, be careful about the amount and language of the after-sales service. If you cannot offer after-sales service in the same EEA State as the customer, or if the service will be in a different language from that of the EEA State, then be clear about this.

EEA States are:

Austria	Greece	Netherlands
Belgium	Hungary	Norway
Bulgaria	Iceland	Poland
Cyprus	Ireland	Portugal
Czech Republic	Italy	Romania
Denmark	Latvia	Slovakia
Estonia	Liechtenstein	Slovenia
Finland	Lithuania	Spain
France	Luxembourg	Sweden
Germany	Malta	United Kingdom

2.9 Offence – CAP Code Section 3

"Marketing communications must not contain anything that is likely to cause serious or widespread offence. Particular care must be taken to avoid causing offence on the grounds of race, religion, gender, sexual orientation, disability or age. Compliance will be judged on the context, medium, audience, product and prevailing standards"[10].

Communications can be distasteful without falling foul of this rule. Note the rule is "serious or widespread offence" – a communication can offend a section of people without falling foul of this rule.

The overall rule is to think about whether you may cause offence and to whom. If you are selling adult products, your communications must be clearly targeted and only available to adults.

www.bmore.co.uk

January 2013
This design company website stated "Who said good creativity should cost an.." next to a picture of an amputee with one arm and leg. Although the ad was targeted at healthcare professionals, the ASA judged that it was easily accessible to the public and could cause serious offence.

---

10 **Source:** CAP Code Section 4 Harm and Offence

Avoid creating fear and distress without justifiable reason, and then be sure not to cause excessive fear or distress. Be careful when referring to anyone who is dead as this may cause distress.

Never appear to encourage or condone violent and anti-social acts. In particular, never encourage drinking and driving.

Do not include any visual effects or techniques that might affect people with photosensitive epilepsy.

> **Hi Spirits: The Antica Sambuca**
>
> **January 2013**
> The company's UK Facebook page, www.facebook.com/AnticaSambucaUK/photos, showed a number of photos which appeared to have been taken in a bar or nightclub and featured young adults holding or consuming alcoholic drinks including shots of Antica Sambuca. In two of the photos a man was shown holding multiple drinks and car keys. In the bottom corner of each photograph was an emblem which stated "Pick 'n' Twist".
>
> Hi Spirits asserted that the photographs were not advertising, nor a sales promotion nor a marketing communication to which the CAP Code applied.
>
> The ASA ruled that the Code did apply as the purpose of the Antica Sambuca Facebook page, including the uploaded images was to promote the brand and the product, and encourage consumers to purchase it.
>
> The ASA ruled the communications breached several parts of the Code. The ASA considered that the images, which included a man holding multiple drinks and car keys, linked alcohol with driving and therefore concluded that they were irresponsible.

2.10 Marketing alcohol – CAP Code Section 18
Never encourage drinking and driving. Where relevant, include a warning about the dangers of drinking and driving.

Never suggest that the effects of drinking alcohol can be masked.

2.11 Marketing to children – CAP Code Section 5
So sensitive is the marketing to children, that an entire section of the CAP code is devoted to it. A child is defined as someone who is under 16 years of age.

"The way in which children perceive and react to marketing communications is influenced by their age, experience and the context in which the message is delivered. Marketing communications that are acceptable for young teenagers will not necessarily be acceptable for younger children. The ASA will take those factors into account when assessing whether a marketing communication complies with the Code."[11]

The first part of the Code looks at ensuring children are not shown in harmful situations. When depicting children in advertising, they must be seen to be safe and acting safely, for example, pedestrians and cyclists must be seen to observe the Highway Code. Specifically, do not:

- encourage children to enter strange places, talk to strangers, or copy practices that might be unsafe to a child;
- do not show children in hazardous situations or behaving dangerously, unless you are promoting safety.

Distance selling marketers must take care when using youth media not to promote products that are unsuitable for children.

---
[11] **Source:** CAP Code, Section 5, Marketing to Children

Trinity Mirror plc

November 2012
A press ad for an online casino, seen in the Daily Mirror, stated "FREE £5 TO PLAY WITH TODAY" and featured a number of cartoon characters, including Optimus Prime from Transformers.

The Advertiser argued that the ad stated participants must be over 18.

The ASA ruled that marketing communications of gambling products should not be likely to be of particular appeal to children or young people, especially by reflecting or being associated with youth culture. The ASA considered that the depiction of the popular comic book characters was likely to have particular appeal to children and young people, regardless of the context in which it appeared.

Peer pressure
Children are vulnerable to wanting to be part of the in-crowd and marketers must not exploit this. You cannot exploit children's credulity, loyalty, vulnerability or lack of experience.

Specifically, you cannot make children feel inferior or unpopular if they do not buy the advertised product, nor can you make them feel that they are being uncourageous, undutiful or disloyal if they do not buy the product.

Under new guidance on using children in peer-to-peer marketing, you cannot make a child feel unpopular, inferior, disloyal, uncourageous or undutiful if the child does not participate in peer-to-peer marketing (encouraging friends to buy the product).[12]

---

12 **Source:** http://www.cap.org.uk/News-reports/Media-Centre/2012/~/media/Files/CAP/Reports%20and%20surveys/CAP%20Review%20brand%20ambassadors%20and%20peer%20to%20peer.ashx

You must make it easy for children to judge the size, performance and characteristics of an advertised product. Children must be able to easily distinguish between real-life and fantasy situations.

Children cannot commit to buying complex or costly products without adult permission.

You may not exaggerate what an ordinary child can attain by using the product.

You may not exploit children's susceptibility to charitable appeals. For charity-linked promotions, you must explain the extent that their participation will help the charity.

Direct exhortation

You may not actively encourage a child to make a nuisance of themselves to encourage parents to buy the product. Note the word 'actively'. You must not undermine parental authority.

You must not directly exhort children to buy or to persuade an adult to buy a product for them. You cannot ask a child to buy something in order to enter a promotion. You cannot target a direct response mechanism to buy a product at children.

Promotion

The rules are not very different from the rules of sales promotions to adults:

- promotions must include a prominent closing date, unless the promotion is a particular pack of the product;
- you must not exaggerate the value of a prize or the chances of winning it.

The main difference is that you must make clear that adult permission is required if a prize/incentive might cause conflict between a child's desire and a parent's (or other adult's) authority, for example prizes such as animals, bicycles, tickets for outings, holidays or concerts.

Distance selling: you cannot target a direct response mechanism to buy a product at children.

Outdoor advertising: while not part of the CAP Code, the The Outdoor Media Centre (OMC) Charter prohibits the display of alcohol advertising within a 100 metre radius of any school entrance, and the display of advertising on static sites for lap dancing clubs or sex shops within 100m of schools or other sensitive locations such as churches and mosques[13].

Advertising food to children

Generally advertisements must not disparage good dietary practice and must avoid anything likely to encourage poor nutritional habits or an unhealthy lifestyle, especially in children.

Food advertisements (except those for fresh fruit or fresh vegetables) targeted at pre-school or primary school children must not include licensed characters or celebrities popular with children.

Note that any brand characters (puppets, persons or characters) that the advertiser has created may be used to sell the products they were designed to sell. Bob the Builder could not be used to sell a breakfast cereal but Kellogg's may use Snap, Crackle and Pop characters.

Checklist for marketing to children[14]
Do:
- Be sensitive to their age, vulnerability and lack of experience
- Tell them to get adult approval if the product is pricey or complex
- Make it easy to judge size, characteristics and performance of a product
- Include the price if the product costs £30 or more

---

13 **Source:** http://check.uk.com/outdoor.html

14 **Source:** http://www.check.uk.com/sales-promotions.html, partially adapted

Don't:
- Make a direct appeal to children to buy advertised products
- Ask them to persuade their parents (or other adults) to buy on their behalf, this is 'pester-power'
- Undermine parental authority (for example "using this is more important than tidying your room")
- Show, encourage or cause any dangerous or immoral behaviour
- Imply children will be unpopular or disloyal if they do not buy the product or peer-to-peer market the product
- Use ambiguous language such as 'only', when you include a price
- Advertise age-inappropriate products (such as alcohol or gaming)
- Invite the child to enter a sales promotion if there is a cost

If you are planning to market to children, use CHECK, the Children's Ethical Communications Kit. It contains rules, legislation and guidance about marketing and communicating to children. CHECK is an Advertising Association initiative, in partnership with Turner Media Innovations and is developed with the help of the entire advertising industry. Go to http://www.check.uk.com.

2.12 Privacy – CAP Code Section 6
Individuals
"Individuals should be protected from unwarranted infringements of privacy."[15]

- Do not use people's details or photos without their written permission, unless you are using a crowd-shot in a general public location.

- Do not unfairly portray or refer to someone in an adverse or offensive way without written permission.

---
[15] **Source:** CAP Code, Section 6 Privacy

- Do not refer to members of the Royal Family or royal properties without permission.

If you use impersonators or caricatures of real people, be careful that it is obviously not the real person and that you are not being offensive[16].

Equi-Sport Horse boxes

September 2012
A photograph of a green and silver horse van appeared on www.equi-sport.co.uk. The licence plate was visible.

The owner of the van complained that his written permission had not been obtained. ASA upheld the complaint.

Property
You can use general public locations without permission as long as they do not denigrate the building or area in question. Frequently used examples include the Houses of Parliament, the Millennium Stadium, Edinburgh Castle and Stormont Castle[17].

2.13 Sales promotions – CAP Code Section 8
The rules apply to all sales promotions, both to consumers and to trade. Sales promotion examples are 'two for the price of one', money-off offers, text-to-win, instant-wins, competitions and prize draws.

Overall, you must deal fairly with participants and avoid causing unnecessary disappointment. Product samples and any promotional items must be safe. Necessary safety advice must be included. You cannot encourage excessive consumption or irresponsible use.

---

16 **Source:** http://www.cap.org.uk/Advice-Training-on-the-rules/Advice-Online-Database/Privacy-Use-of-impersonators-and-caricatures.aspx

17 **Source:** http://www.cap.org.uk/Advice-Training-on-the-rules/Advice-Online-Database/Privacy-Landmarks-and-property.aspx

As with other areas of the CAP code, you cannot promote alcohol to under 18s, nor should you cause serious or widespread offence.

Availability: to your best estimate, you should be capable of meeting the likely response. If you do run out, you must offer either a refund or an equivalent product.

Significant conditions: all significant conditions must be communicated. If there is insufficient space for all the specific conditions, then you must make it clear where the information is available.

Significant conditions include:

- How to participate
- Any free entry route
- Start date
- Closing date. It is not compulsory to have a closing date: you can say "subject to availability" (such as special purchase packs of products) but then you must have a reasonable amount of the product available
- Proof of purchase details
- Prizes and gifts
- Any restrictions, such as age or geographic or internet access
- Promoter's name and address
- Any restrictions on the number of entries
- Whether the promoter can substitute a cash alternative
- Date when prize will be distributed, if more than 30 days after the closing date
- How and when winners will be notified of results
- How and when information about winners and results will be made available – prizewinners must not be compromised by publication of excessive personal information
- Any intention to use winners in post-event publicity

Prizes: you cannot say someone is a winner if they are not. You cannot exaggerate the chances of winning. You should use the laws of chance to allocate the prizes – in other words, prizes must be awarded fairly.

Competitions: if there is an element of judgement in awarding the prize, you must be clear what this is and the judges must be independent.

Trade incentives: must not compromise the obligation of employees to give honest advice to consumers. It must be clear if a tax liability might arise.

Charity-linked promotions
You must:

- name each charity or cause that will benefit and have a formal agreement
- if not a registered charity, define its nature and objectives
- specify exactly what will be gained by a named charity and state the basis on which the contribution will be calculated
- state any limits on contributions
- not exaggerate the benefits to the charity
- if the promotion states, or implies, part of the price paid will be given to the charity, then state the actual amount or % of the price that will be paid
- if asked, make available to consumers a current or final total of contributions made
- not directly encourage children to buy, or exhort children to persuade an adult to buy for them, a product that promotes charitable purposes. Note the words 'directly encourage' here.

2.14 Distance selling – CAP Code Section 9 – see Chapter 3

2.15 Data protection – CAP Code Section 10 – see Chapter 5

2.16 Political advertisements – CAP Code Section 7
Advertisements to influence voters in local, national, international or referendum votes are not included in the CAP code.

Advertisements by central government, not relating to party policy, are covered by the Code.

2.17 Other CAP rules for specialised areas
These specialised areas are beyond the scope of this Handbook. There are rules on the marketing of:

- medicines, medical devices, treatments and health
- weight control and slimming
- food, food supplements
- financial products
- faith, religion
- charities
- gambling
- lotteries
- alcohol
- motoring
- betting tipsters
- introduction and dating services
- private investigation agencies

If these apply to you, please check the relevant areas of the CAP code.

Chapter 3: Distance Selling[18]

Distance selling promotes specific goods and services, including direct response mechanisms, allowing readers to place orders without face-to-face contact with the marketer.[19]

Distance Selling is covered by a number of codes and legislation: in addition to Section 9 of the CAP code there are the Consumer Protection (Distance Selling) Regulations 2000 (as amended).

In addition, the DMA (Direct Marketing Association) has its own DM Code of Practice which its members must observe.[20] This includes some practices not covered by CAP. This chapter attempts to cover all the practices which are likely to be relevant for the marketer.

BCAP also has specific requirements for broadcast distance selling advertisements and these are included at the end of the chapter.

Distance Selling Regulations (DSR) and Electronic Commerce (EC Directive) Regulations 2002 (ECR)
Overview
The Regulations give consumers a right to:

- receive clear information about the supplier, the goods or services and the sale before deciding to buy;
- confirmation of this information in writing;
- a cancellation period of 7 working days in which to withdraw from the contract; and
- protection from payment card fraud.

---

18 **Sources:** http://www.out-law.com, http://www.compactlaw.co.uk/free-legal-articles/distance-selling-regs-2000.html, https://www.gov.uk/online-and-distance-selling-for-businesses;

http://www.southend.gov.uk/info/200098/trading_standards/1066/selling_on_the_internet/3

19 **Source:** adapted from CAP Code, Section 9 Distance Selling

20 **Source:** www.dma.org.uk

Note: a new EU Rights Directive comes into force EU wide by the end of 2013. The new directive harmonises consumer rights protection across the EU for all business to customer (B2C) online sales of goods and services. Items here marked with a ◆ will be enforced by this legislation.[21]

Does it affect me?
They do not affect B2B sales.

They affect marketers who sell goods and services to consumers without face-to-face contact. It includes selling via the internet, email, text messaging, telephone, fax, interactive TV and mail order.

If you normally do business face-to-face, DSR will not apply to an occasional order taken at a distance. DSRs only apply if you routinely sell at a distance.

The Regulations do not apply to:

- most contracts for the sale or transfer of land or for building on land, except short rental agreements;
- contracts for the supply of financial services;
- automated vending machines (for example pictures taken from an automated photo booth);
- contracts by telephone through the use of public pay-phones; or
- contracts concluded at auction (it must be a genuine auction in order to qualify for the exemption. 'Buy it now' slots on internet auction sites, such as Ebay, are not exempt).

How does it work?
It sets out information you must give consumers. You are required to refund customers in a certain time and you must perform the contract (provide the goods or service) within a reasonable time.

---

21 **Source:** http://www.bodlelaw.com/e-commerce/website-legal-requirements-online-sales-new-consumer-rights

Information you must provide[22]

Before an order is placed, you must display:

- your business name and geographic address. The address must be a real address, a PO Box number will not do;
- a description of your goods or services;
- the price, including all taxes and delivery charges;
- how a customer can pay;
- delivery arrangements, costs and how long goods will take to arrive. Goods should arrive within 30 days of the consumer sending their order (unless it is reasonable to take longer, such as made-to-measure products, or plants that are out of season);
- the minimum length of the contract;
- for contracts of over one year or open-ended contracts, conditions for terminating the contract; and
- information about the customer's right to cancel (usually within 7 clear working days after delivery (see refunds below) ◆ this will be increased to 14 days, can be for no reason, and must be free of charge to the customer.

It is also good practice to explain who pays for returning goods if the customer cancels.

◆ If a contract is cancelled during the cooling-off period, provided that the goods are returned within 14 days of the customer giving notice of cancellation, the supplier must refund:

- the price within 14 days of the cancellation date; and
- the postage costs for returning the goods, unless the supplier clearly informed the customer prior to the contract being concluded, that these costs would not be refunded.

---

22 **Source:** https://www.gov.uk/online-and-distance-selling-for-businesses

After an order is placed: in good time after an order is placed, and no later than the delivery of the goods, you must provide your customer in writing with:

- how and when they can cancel an order and who pays for returning goods
- an address where complaints can be sent
- any guarantees or after-sales services you offer; and
- conditions for terminating contracts of over 1 year or open-ended contracts.

'In writing' means a form the customer can keep such as an email, a letter or a set of printed terms and conditions.

Online sellers
If you sell goods online, you must also:

- list the steps involved in a customer placing an order
- acknowledge receipt of any orders as soon as possible
- make it easy for customers to check their orders and correct any errors, and explain how to do so
- let customers know what languages are available to them
- make sure customers can store and reproduce your terms and conditions. Terms and conditions should be readily accessible, fair and meaningful
- give your email address and VAT number (if your business is registered for VAT)
- for marketers of services, make it clear when the services will begin
- state any telephone, postal or other communication charges calculated at higher than the standard rate (for example, if a premium-rate call is required)

- for a promotion, state how long the offer will last
- provide a statement on whether the marketer intends to provide substitute products (of equivalent quality and price) if those ordered are unavailable. If a substitute will be provided, a statement explaining that if the substitute is not acceptable, the cost of returning the substitute product will be refunded
- ◆ make clear the total price, including all charges before the online sale is concluded. The use of 'pre-ticked boxes' to conceal hidden charges will no longer be acceptable.

Which regulation applies:[23]

	DSRs	ECRs
The internet	Y	Y
Email	Y	Y
Text messaging	Y	Y
Video and picture messaging	Y	
Telephone	Y	
Fax	Y	
Interactive TV	Y	Y
Mail order - catalogues	Y	
Mail order - advertising in newspapers, magazines	Y	

---

23 **Source:** Distance Selling Explained – guidance for those selling via website, telephone or mail order. Published by the Office of Fair Trading, edition 02/12, available from http://dshub.tradingstandards.gov.uk

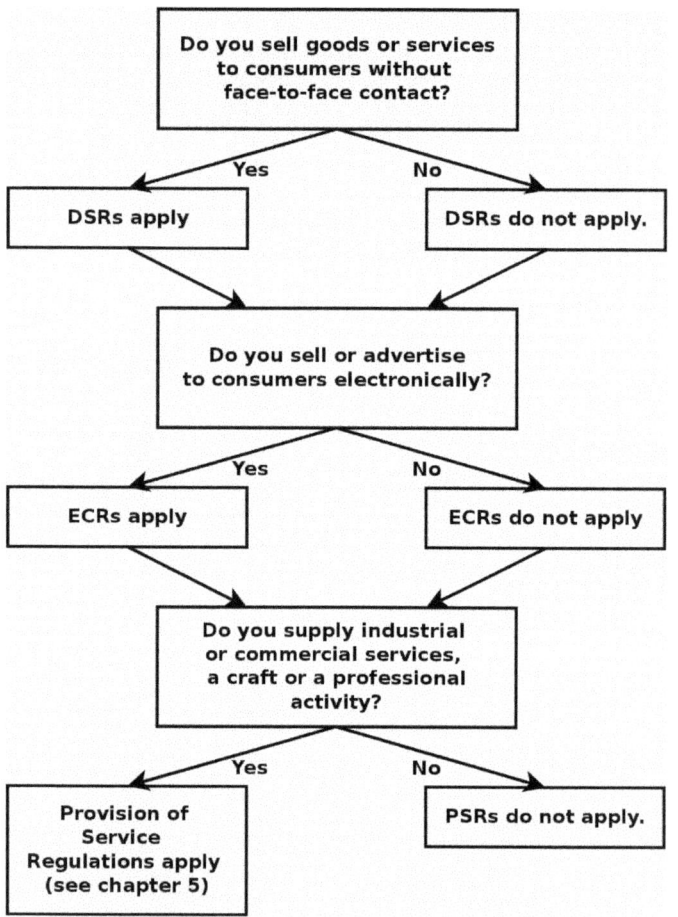

Figure 3.1 Which distance selling regulations apply?[24]

---

[24] **Source:** Distance Selling Explained – guidance for those selling via website, telephone or mail order. Published by the Office of Fair Trading, edition 02/12, available from http://dshub.tradingstandards.gov.uk

Refunds

You must refund the consumer promptly (within 30 days' notice of cancellation) if:

- consumers have not received products within the specified period. If they prefer to wait, consumers must be given a firm dispatch date or fortnightly progress reports. Alternatively you may provide a substitute of equivalent quality and price;
- products are returned because they are damaged, faulty or not as described; you must pay for delivery and return;
- consumers cancel within seven clear working days after delivery (◆ increased to 14 days). Note: consumers may try out products, except for audio or video recordings or computer software, but should take reasonable care of them. If trying out the product, consumers must return the product and pay the costs of returning;
- an unconditional money-back guarantee is given and the products are returned within a reasonable period; and
- the consumer can produce proof of posting even if returned products are not received back by the company.

You must inform customers of their right to withdraw from the contract within the cooling-off period. The cooling-off period is currently 7 days and will extend to 14 days; otherwise the customer's right to withdraw will automatically extend to 12 months.

You do not have to provide a refund if:

- services have already begun with the consumer's agreement
- the price of the product depends on financial market fluctuations outside the control of the supplier
- or:
    - on perishable, personalised or made-to-measure products
    - on audio or video recordings or computer software if unsealed by the consumer
    - on newspapers, periodicals or magazines
    - on betting, gaming or lottery services

Other issues
Packaging: take care when packaging products that might fall into the hands of children.

Unsolicited products: you cannot ask consumers to pay for or return unsolicited products.

You cannot falsely claim a consumer ordered a product by including an invoice in the marketing materials.

Surcharges and 'Hotlines': suppliers must not charge customers more for specific payment methods than they pay themselves, such as fees for using a credit or charge card. In addition customer service telephone numbers must be charged at a basic rate: premium rate is not permitted.

BCAP additional requirements for broadcast distance selling advertisements
Broadcasters have the responsibility for ensuring that the advertiser will comply with the rules for distance selling. In particular, the broadcaster must ensure that the advertiser:

- can take enquiries during normal business hours,
- has made adequate arrangements to protect the consumers' money,
- can give refunds,
- will inform consumers about cancellation rights.

> # Chapter 4: Product Placement (Ofcom Broadcasting Code)[25]

Product placement is when a company pays a TV channel or a programme-maker to include its products or brands in a programme. Examples include a fashion company paying for a presenter to wear its clothes during a programme, or a car manufacturer might pay for a character to mention one of its cars in a drama.

Overview

Product placement in films and international programmes is now allowed on UK television. Since February 2011, radio and TV programmes made for UK audiences may include product placement in drama, entertainment, games shows, soap operas and sports shows. It is not allowed in children's, religious, news or documentary programmes or on BBC shows.

Does it affect me?

Only if you do, or intend to, advertise your products through product placement on TV or radio shows.

How does it work? [26]

Paid for placements must be flagged as such to the TV audience or radio listener. On television, a logo is used. The logo must be shown before and after the show and repeated after any advertising break during the programme. For radio, the broadcasters must ensure that listeners are made aware that commercial references are paid for.

---

25 **Source:** Ofcom Broadcasting Code can be found at stakeholders.ofcom.org.uk/broadcasting/broadcast-codes/broadcast-code

26 **Sources:** "I'm not a lawyer, but...." published by the CIM;

http://www.bjretaillaw.com/resource/product-placement/;

http://consumers.ofcom.org.uk/2011/02/product-placement-on-tv/

Product placement logo

Product placement must not 'impair broadcasters' and must be editorially justified. This means that programmes cannot be created or distorted so that they are vehicles for featuring product placements. Note that products are 'placed', not overtly promoted, so you cannot have characters saying how good they are or have so many references to the product that the audience feels the product is being promoted.

What cannot be product placed:

- products that cannot be legally advertised on British TV, such as weapons or escort agencies
- no tobacco, alcohol, gambling or food/drinks high in fat, salt or sugar
- no medicines
- no baby milk

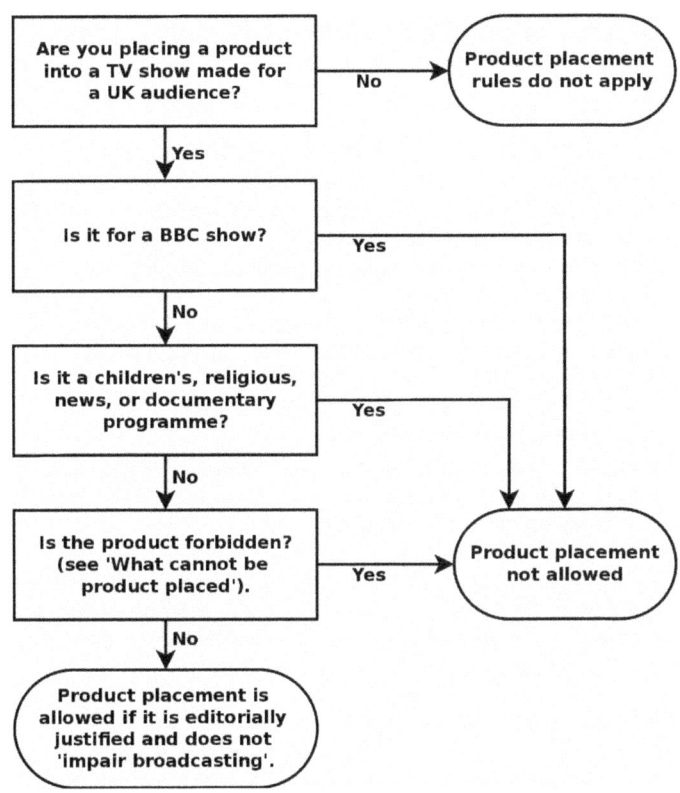

Figure 4.1 Product placement

Chapter 5: Provision of Services Regulations 2009 (PSR)[27]

Overview
The PSR applies to most businesses that provide a service to a consumer or another business. It mainly concerns what information you must provide for your customer and how to deal with complaints. It also states that you cannot refuse to supply your services based on the geographic location of a consumer, except under set criteria.

Handling complaints under PSR is straightforward and standard good practice. Supplying the information required is not onerous and can be done on your website.

Does it affect me?
If you are offering services that are paid for, they are likely to apply to you. The PSR apply to services for consumers or businesses and whether agreed face-to-face or at a distance.

The PSR do not apply to selling or making goods, so most retailers are exempt. But the regulations do apply to any after-sales service or customer advice, so if you are a computer shop that also does repairs, then the PSR apply.

Services that are covered include:

- services provided to both businesses and to consumers; for example, estate agents, construction services, restaurants, storage services, financial advisers
- consumer services; for example, tourism, leisure services, child minders, private schools and universities, driving instructors, cleaners

---

[27] **Sources:** http://dshub.tradingstandards.gov.uk/; http://www.startups.co.uk/provision-of-services-regulations.html; http://www.lawson-west.co.uk/lawyers-for-business/business-law-disputes/Provision-Services-Regs/

- business services; for example, advertising, waste management, training, professional services such as lawyers and accountants

The PSR do not apply if your business is:

- financial services; for example banks, credit card providers, insurance providers
- electronic communications services and network providers
- transport services; for example, flights, rail travel. However, they do apply to removal services, car rental services, driving instructors, MOT service centres, funeral services and aerial photography services
- services of temporary work agencies
- healthcare services, both public and private
- audiovisual services; for example, cinemas and broadcast services
- gambling services
- social services provided by the State, by providers mandated by the State, or by charities recognised as such by the State. However, they do apply to services provided on a commercial basis by registered charitable organisations or their trading subsidiaries
- private security services
- services provided by notaries and bailiffs

How does it work?

Information requirements
The PSR require you to supply information to your customers clearly and unambiguously. The information you must supply is:

- the name of your business
- the main features of the service
- your legal status (for example sole trader, limited company)
- your geographic address and contact details (where appropriate, an email address or number for text messages)

- your trade, or public register name, and registration number details of any authorisation scheme in the UK or an EEA state (for list of EEA states, see section 2.8)
- VAT identification number
- if you are in a regulated profession, your professional title, professional body or similar institution you are registered with and the EEA state in which that title has been granted
- your general terms and conditions
- any after-sales guarantee (that is not already imposed by law)
- the price of the service if a price is pre-determined
- information about any professional liability insurance or guarantee, including the contact details of the insurer or guarantor and the territorial coverage
- how to access details of non-judicial dispute resolution procedures if you are subject to a code of conduct or are a member of a trade association or professional body that gives access to such procedures

You must use one of these methods to make this information available:

- simply supply it to the customer
- make it easily accessible to the customer at the place where the service is provided or the contract is concluded, for example, at your premises
- make it easily accessible by the customer electronically, for example, giving the customer details of a website where the information is published
- include it in any information documents that you supply

For an example of how a company has supplied this information, see Savills estate agent[28]:

---

[28] **Source:** www.savills.co.uk/footer/provision-of-services-regulations.aspx

Name	**Savills (UK) Limited**
Legal status	A limited liability company registered in England & Wales
Service offering	Details of the service we provide can be found at: http://www.savills.com/services
Registered office and postal address	33 Margaret Street, London, W1G 0JD
Email	westend@savills.com
Telephone	+44 (0) 20 7499 8644
Public registers	Details about the company registration can be viewed at www.companieshouse.gov.uk under company number 2605138.
Consumer credit licence	Details of our consumer credit licence can be found at www2.crw.gov.uk/pr and our licence number is 372813. Any complaint regarding services provided under this licence can be made to the Financial Services Ombudsman at http://www.financial-ombudsman.org.uk
VAT number	577 6575 79
General terms and conditions	A letter of engagement accompanied by our standard terms and conditions will be provided to the client at the commencement of any engagement to which they apply.
Applicable law	Unless otherwise agreed, English law, with the English Courts having exclusive jurisdiction in relation to any claim, dispute or difference concerning the service and any matter arising from it.

Insurance	In accordance with the disclosure requirements of the Provision of Services Regulations 2009, our professional indemnity insurance is arranged by Windsor Partners Limited of 71 Fenchurch Street, London EC3M 4BS. The policies comply with the requirements of the RICS and the FSA and the territorial and jurisdictional cover is worldwide, subject always to the full terms and conditions of the policy.
Regulation	We are members of the Royal Institution of Chartered Surveyors (RICS). For residential lettings we are members of the Association of Residential Letting Agents (ARLA). We are authorised and regulated by the Financial Services Authority (FSA) in respect of insurance mediation activity. Details of our registration with the FSA can be viewed at http://www.fsa.gov.uk/register/home.do under reference number 442478.
Complaints	Complaints: We operate a formal procedure to deal with complaints from clients and others. Details of this procedure are available from the Customer Relations Officer at complaints@savills.com. We are also members of the Ombudsman Services: Property, which provides for the resolution of any consumer complaints that are not satisfactorily resolved between the parties to be referred to the independent Ombudsman. The Ombudsman Services: Property website is: www.os-property.org. For unresolved business to business complaints there are provisions for matters to be referred to mediation or arbitration as appropriate.

Table 5.1 Provision of Services Regulations, Savills (UK) Limited

Additionally, if your customers ask for this information, you must provide:

- the price of the service. If an exact price cannot be given, the method for calculating the price so that it can be checked by the recipient, or a detailed estimate
- if you are in a regulated profession, a reference to the professional rules applicable in your EEA state and how to easily access them – for example, on a website
- information on any other activities carried out by you or your business that are directly linked to the service in question, and on the measures taken to avoid conflicts of interest
- any codes of conduct governing you, and the websites from which these codes are available, specifying the language version available

Complaints

You must respond to all complaints from customers as quickly as possible. Under the information required (see above) you need to give details of how to make a complaint.

For all genuine complaints, you should try to find a satisfactory solution. You may ignore complaints that are 'vexatious', which are complaints that are clearly unsubstantiated or frivolous. Note, that an annoying or inconvenient complaint may still be genuine!

Non-discrimination over place of customer's residence[29]

This applies to your general terms and conditions for individual consumers, not companies.

If you operate in the UK and are based in the UK or an EEA state, you may not discriminate against individual customers depending on their location (town, country or region).

---

29 **Source:** http://www.baineswilson.co.uk/pdfs/12.01.10 The Provisions of Services Regulations1.pdf

This means you cannot simply refuse to supply your service, offer different terms or provide a different service simply based on the customer's place of residence.

You can have different conditions based on 'objective criteria' such as lack of adequate Intellectual Property protection, or additional costs due to the distance travelled or technical characteristics of the service. So, for example, you could charge a higher price to cover travel costs.

You can refuse to supply services to a location if you can prove that this would put 'excessive strain' on your business.

Chapter 6: Data Protection[30]

Data Protection rules are covered in the CAP Code, the Data Protection Act and The Privacy and Electronic Communications Regulations (PECR). PECR were amended on 26 May 2011 to include the so-called 'Cookie Law'.

6.1 Data Protection Act 1998[31]
Overview
The Data Protection Act aims to ensure that a person's data held by a company is held honestly and fairly.

Does it apply to me?
If you handle personal information about living people, then yes, it does.

Personal data includes, among other things:

- Names
- Addresses
- E-mail addresses
- Telephone numbers
- Location data
- IP addresses
- Expressions of opinion about individuals
- CCTV images

In certain circumstances, it can include anonymised or aggregated data.

---

[30] **Sources:** http://www.ico.gov.uk/for_organisations/privacy_and_electronic_communications.aspx; http://ico.org.uk/for_organisations/sector_guides/marketing

[31] **Sources:** http://www.backupdirect.net/data-protection-act-summary; http://uk.practicallaw.com/4-385-3476

Some personal data is sensitive, including details about:

- Health
- Criminal record
- Sexual orientation
- Trade union membership
- Racial or ethnic origin
- Political or religious views

How does it work?
There are 8 principles that you must comply with. If you follow the spirit of these, you are likely to be compliant with the Act. Essentially, you must be honest with the individuals whose data you hold and be fair with their data.

1. Data must be processed fairly and lawfully.	Any personal data collected must be provided with the individual's consent. You must be transparent about why you are collecting it.
2. Information collected must be processed for limited purposes.	You can only use data in the way you said you would. So if you collect data for market research, you cannot then use it for direct mailing the individual without getting their permission first.
3. Information collected must be adequate, relevant and not excessive.	Only ask for and hold data that is relevant to your company. Do not collect data that you think might come in useful in the future.
4. Information collected must be accurate and up to date.	
5. Information must not be held for longer than is necessary.	Conduct regular reviews of personal data and do not hoard information that is no longer needed.

6. Information must be processed in accordance with the individual's rights.	The individual has a right of access to their data. S/he also has a right to have inaccurate data corrected or erased or destroyed. S/he can object to having his/her data processed and for having data used for direct marketing.
7. Information must be kept secure.	You have a duty to keep data safe. Common breaches of this are when organisations lose data on a laptop.
8. Information should not be transferred outside the European Economic Area (EEA) unless adequate levels of protection exist.	If you plan to hold data overseas, you must gain the individual's consent. You must also ensure that the data will be safe and that there are safe harbouring laws.

Council fined £250,000 after employee records found in supermarket car park recycle bin

11 September 2012

A Council whose former employees' pension records were found in an over-filled paper recycle bank in a supermarket car park have been fined £250,000 for the data breach.

Scottish Borders Council employed an outside company to digitise the records, but failed to seek appropriate guarantees on how the personal data would be kept secure....It is believed more than 600 files were deposited at the recycle bins, containing confidential information and, in a significant number of cases, salary and bank account details.

Source: http://www.backupdirect.net/council-fined-250000-after-employee-records-found-in-supermarket-car-park-recycle-bin-11092012

6.2 The Privacy and Electronic Communications Regulations (PECR)

Overview

This includes the so called the 'cookie' law but it applies to any form of marketing communications sent electronically to individuals (so all B2C and B2B if sent to sole traders).

Does it affect me?

Cookie rules apply if your website uses cookies – which is most websites (see section 6.6).

If you process personal data for marketing, you will need to comply with both the Data Protection Act and The Privacy and Electronic Communications Regulations (PECR). It is good practice to comply with both even if not strictly necessary.

PECR apply to all B2C marketing communications, and B2B if addressed to sole traders and partners in business partnerships, because these are seen as individuals. Rules for communicating with corporates are slightly different (see section 6.3).

PECR apply if you are sending marketing and advertising by electronic means such as by telephone, fax, email, text message, picture (including video) message, and by using an automated calling system.

If you know the name of the person you are targeting, then you must also comply with the Data Protection Act.

If you do not know the person's name (for example, you just have a list of telephone numbers), then you do not need to comply with the Data Protection Act. However, you must comply with the Data Protection Act as soon as you do know the person's name.

Electronic mail[32]

What is electronic mail:

- email
- text
- picture marketing messages
- video marketing messages
- marketing transmitted in WAP messages, including WAP Push voicemail and answerphone messages left by marketers making marketing calls that would otherwise be 'live'. WAP Push allows a sender to send a specially formatted SMS message to a handset. With a single click, the receiver can then access and view content stored online, through the browser on the handset.

Fax messages are not included (see section 6.4).

If you are carrying out electronic marketing, you must:

- check you have that person's consent
- identify your company
- provide a valid address for the recipient to send an opt out request. For a text marketing message, this could be a short number to text

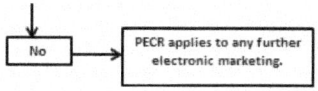

---

[32] **Source:**

http://www.ico.org.uk/for_organisations/privacy_and_electronic_communications/the_guide/electronic_mail

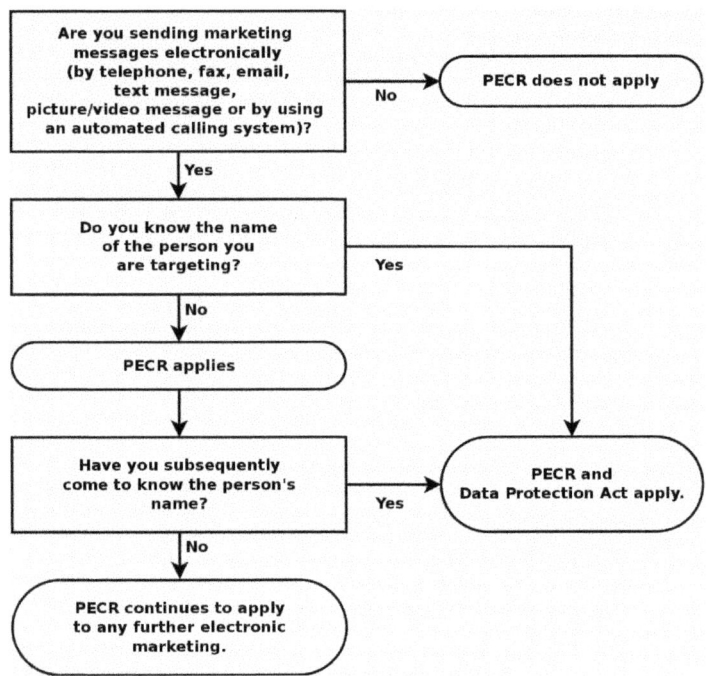

Figure 6.1 PECR Checklist

How does it work?
Solicited and unsolicited marketing
A solicited marketing message is actively invited. This invitation can be given via a third party, such as another company in your group or a reseller.

An unsolicited marketing message is any other email that the receiver has not invited but not indicated they object to receiving. If challenged, you would need to demonstrate that the subscriber has positively opted in to receiving further information from you.

Consent
There are two levels of consent: opt-in and opt-out. For some marketing communications you need to have opt-in, that is explicit consent to contact the person with a marketing message – unless you have this consent, you may not market to them. For other marketing communications, you can simply check whether a person has opted-out, that is said that they do not wish to receive this type of communication. If they have not opted out, then you may market to them until they tell you to stop.

	Opt-in Specific consent must be held by your company	Opt-out Assume you can contact them but check if they have opted out
Direct mail		X
Telemarketing		X
Marketing messages left on voicemail and answer machine	X	
Fax marketing		X
Electronic communications (text, WAP, picture)	X	
Email marketing message	X	

If you want to carry out electronic marketing, you must have the permission of the person you are marketing to. This must be given 'knowingly' so that the person understands that they are consenting to receive marketing material.

Ways that you can obtain this consent include getting the person:

a) to tick a box
b) to click on an icon
c) to subscribe to a service
d) not to opt out of receiving marketing messages, provided the wording is clear. For example:

"By submitting this registration form, you will be indicating your consent to receiving email marketing messages from us unless you have indicated an objection to receiving such messages by ticking the above box."

You cannot assume someone has consented just because they have not ticked a box to opt-out.

However, you can use a 'soft opt-in' which is where:

- you have obtained a person's details in the course of a sale or negotiation for a product or service
- you are marketing a similar product or service
- the person is given a simple opportunity to refuse marketing when their details are collected
- the person is given a simple way to refuse marketing in future marketing messages

Charities: the soft opt-in only applies to commercial organisations. So it does apply to a charity's trading arm but does not apply to charity supporters.

6.3 E-mail marketing – legal requirements[33]

Currently, solicited or unsolicited e-mail (or text messaging) marketing must state:

- that the e-mail or text message is a commercial communication;
- the name of the company/or person on whose behalf the communication is being sent; and
- if appropriate, that the communication is a promotional offer (including any discount, premium or gift) or promotional competition or game.

The rules for corporate subscribers

You can send an unsolicited marketing email to a corporate subscriber, but not a sole trader or partner. Sole traders and partners in partnerships are seen as individuals.

You must take care to ascertain that it really is a corporate email (x@y.co.uk email addresses may be personal ones, but an email to sales@, or helpdesk@ or info@ are clearly corporate). Marketing emails sent to a named individual at a company email are permitted if they are clearly work related (for example promoting office facilities) but not if it is personal (for example promoting family holidays).

What is consent?

Consent must be positive, for example, the consumer must tick a box or an icon, send an email or subscribe to a service. The key issue is to make sure that the consumer understands they are giving consent and what they are agreeing to.

---

[33] **Source:** http://www.bodlelaw.com/e-commerce/website-legal-requirements-data-commissioner-fines-for-unsolicited-e-mails

> **Good practice recommendations from the information commissioner**
>
> Try to go for permission-based marketing as much as possible. This way you are only contacting customers who want you to contact them.
> - Provide a statement of use when you collect details. Put this in an obvious place or make sure it has to be read before individuals submit their details.
> - Make sure you clearly explain what individuals' details will be used for. For example, explain to individuals why you might use their email address in the future.
> - Do not have consent boxes already ticked.
> - Provide a simple and quick method for customers to opt out of marketing messages at no cost other than that of sending the message.
> - Promptly comply with opt-out requests from everyone, not just those from individuals.
> - Have a system in place to deal with complaints about unwanted marketing.
> - When you receive an opt-out request, suppress the individual or company details rather than deleting them. This way you will have a record of who not to contact.
>
> **Source:** Data Protection Good Practice Note published by the Information Commissioner, published 21/12/06

If you trade under different names

If you trade under several different names, particularly where those names are strong brands, you should not assume that a customer who agrees to receive mailing from one trading entity is agreeing to receive marketing from your other trading entities. Customers may not even be aware of any connection between different trading names.

Under the Data Protection Act, if you are collecting personal data, you will need to ensure the different entities are clearly explained to your customers.[34]

6.4 Telemarketing and fax marketing

The Telephone Preference Service (TPS) is operated by the Direct Marketing Association and it allows people to register their telephone number to opt-out of receiving unsolicited calls (http://www.tpsonline.org.uk). There is also a Fax Preference Service (FPS) which does the same for faxes (http://www.fpsonline.org.uk).

You may not do telephone or fax marketing to people who are registered with the TPS or FPS.

If you subcontract your telemarketing or fax marketing, you are still responsible for ensuring that you do not contact telephone numbers registered with the TPS or FPS.

When carrying out telemarketing, the call operator must give the name of the company whose products or services they are promoting. So if you are using a subcontractor, they will identify your company, not the subcontractor.

If the person called asks, the call operator must explain how your company can be contacted with an opt-out request. This may be either a valid address or free phone number.

For fax marketing, the fax must clearly state your company name and either a valid address or free phone number to send an opt-out to.

---

[34] **Source:**

http://www.ico.org.uk/for_organisations/privacy_and_electronic_communications/the_guide/electronic_mail

If a current customer is listed with the TPS and you wish to contact them for marketing:

- you should not call them for marketing unless they have positively told you that you may
- positive ways the customer can tell you include ticking a box, or signing up to a service when you have clearly told the customer this means they do not object to your making marketing calls to them
- you must provide a simple means for the customer to object to receiving calls at any time[35]

Automated calls: these are pre-recorded calls, not calls dialled by an automated calling system or power-dialler. You must have specific permission from the person receiving the call.

6.5 Direct marketing

There is a Mailing Preference Service (MPS) which allows people to limit the amount of direct mail that they receive. If you are planning a direct marketing campaign, you must check your list against the MPS list (http://www.mpsonline.org.uk).

Baby MPS – there is a specific, daily up-dated list that covers baby details. Should a baby die, the last thing the parents need is to receive direct marketing about baby related items. Baby MPS stores this data and allows companies to avoid contacting bereaved parents (http://www.mpsonline.org.uk/bmps/).

---

[35] **Source:** Information Commissioner's Office Privacy and Electronic Communications Guidance Calling customers listed on the TPS 2012/12/12 Version: 1.1

6.6 Cookie law[36]
Overview
Most of the discussion in the media around implementing the PECR was the introduction of the so called 'Cookie Law'.

Cookie Law intends to protect people from any underhand use of cookies to spy on their browsing behaviour. Websites must explain their use of cookies and give visitors the choice to accept or reject cookies.

What is a cookie?
A cookie is a small file of letters and numbers that websites place on their users' computers. These reveal information about the user, such as their browsing behaviour. The reason for the introduction of the rules was that users either did not know that this information was being stored or were not aware that they could opt-out of receiving the cookie.

There are two types of cookie:

1. session cookies which are not stored long-term. These expire once the user finishes a browsing session. These are used to track the pages a user has seen.
2. persistent (tracking) cookies which are stored between browsing sessions, so as to remember user preferences or target advertising.

---

[36] **Sources:** Information Commissioner's Office (May 2012) Guidance on the rules on use of cookies and similar technologies, Guidance on the EU Cookie Law/e-privacy Direct;
http://www.computerweekly.com/tip/How-to-audit-cookies-for-compliance-with-PECR-regulations;
http://www.computerweekly.com/news/2240112940/ICO-stands-by-unpopular-UK-cookie-legislation-with-advice-warnings; http://www.cubik.co.uk/help/get-help/Privacy-and-Electronic-Communications-Regulations; http://www.inpublishing.co.uk/kb/articles/complying_with_the_pecr.aspx

There are also:

- first party cookies set directly by the website
- third party cookies set by other services such as social bookmarking, website analytics and video streaming

Does it affect me?
Yes, if you have a website that uses cookies.

How does it work?
You need to:

- inform users there are cookies on your site
- explain what the cookies are used for
- obtain their consent to store cookies on their device (computer, smart phone, tablet)

Consent is not needed for each individual cookie, provided you have clear consent for the purpose of the cookie (for example, if you have consent for using cookies for analytical purposes, you do not need it for each cookie that is used for analysis).

If you are using cookies only where strictly necessary for your service (such as saving items to a shopping cart), then you do not need to ask for consent. Table 6.1 (adapted from The Information Commissioner's published advice) shows when you do not need to ask for consent:

Consent not needed (activities likely to fall within the exception)	Consent needed (activities unlikely to fall within the exception)
A cookie used to remember the goods a user wishes to buy when they proceed to the checkout or add goods to their shopping basket	Cookies used for analytical purposes to count the number of unique visits to a website for example
If cookies are essential to comply with the seventh data protection principle ("all data must be secure") – for example in connection with online banking services	First and third party advertising cookies
Cookies that help ensure that the content of your page loads quickly and effectively by distributing the workload across numerous computers	Cookies used to recognise a user when they return to a website so that the greeting they receive can be tailored

Table 6.1 Cookie Law

The main method businesses have adopted to comply with the Cookie Law is to use a wording such as:

"We use cookies to ensure that our site works correctly and provides you with the best experience. If you continue using our site without changing your browser settings, we'll assume that you agree to our use of cookies. Find out more about the cookies we use and how to manage them by reading our cookies policy."[37]

One of the issues has been whether just by visiting your website, the visitor gives implied consent to you setting a cookie. The Information Commissioner has decided that it is not sufficient unless you make it very clear to the visitor that this is what is happening. Eventually browser settings may be used by websites to assume implied consent, but at the moment, relying on browser settings is not sufficient.

Visitors can change their mind and refuse consent at any time for cookies and you must make it clear how they can do this.

---

37 **Source:** http://www.phonepayplus.org.uk

6.7 Viral marketing
For many marketers, viral marketing is the wonderful situation when an advert or video goes 'viral' on social media and brings huge corporate recognition. However, this is a Broadcast advertisement (see BCAP Chapter 8).

Under the PECR rules, 'viral marketing' is where:

- you ask a person to send the original marketing message to a friend or friends; or
- you ask a person to give you their friends' contact details.

You may or may not offer an incentive to do so.

In both cases, you are the instigator. In the first case, if you explicitly ask a person to send on the message, you should be very clear that they should only pass on your email to people they are sure will be pleased to receive it. This is obviously good marketing, as you do not want your customers sending your company details to people who are not interested.

When you ask for contact details, you are still liable for ensuring you have consent, so you should:

- ask your customer to confirm that they have the consent of the other person
- check that the other person is not already on your suppression list
- tell your customer that you propose to let the other person know how you got their details

Loyalty schemes
If a customer has joined your loyalty scheme, you can view this as a soft opt-in for you to tell the customer about the amount of points they have and other incentives in the scheme, unless they have opted out of receiving these.

6.8 Public electronic communications service providers

These have specific requirements under the PECR, covering the safety of the data, itemised billing, Caller Line Id, information about users (traffic information) and dealing with anonymous and nuisance calls.

This specialised regulation is outside the scope of this Handbook for general marketers. For further information, see information published by the Information Commissioner:

http://www.ico.org.uk/for_organisations/privacy_and_electronic_communications/the_guide/security_of_services

http://www.ico.org.uk/for_organisations/privacy_and_electronic_communications/the_guide/security_breaches

>/traffic_data

>/location_data

>/itemised_billing

>/connected line identification, /directories of subscribers, /contracts, /national security, /legal requirements

Chapter 7: Premium Rate Telephone Services (PRS)[38]

PRS is regulated by PhonepayPlus through a Code of Practice.

Does it affect me?
Yes, if you use anything other than standard-rate phone calls or text messages to consumers. Such services include TV voting, chat lines, gambling services and charity donations by text message.

Any businesses involved in providing premium rate services to consumers – apart from companies that only provide 0871, 0872 and 0873 numbers – must be registered with PhonepayPlus.

What does it mean?
The Code covers pricing, advertising and promotions.
The Code divides providers into 3 types:

- Network providers
- Level 1 providers who are part of the value-chain
- Level 2 providers who are the end-provider of the service

You can fall into more than one category. The rules that affect Marketers are predominately those for Level 2 providers, as this is the end-provider. A customer may only be aware of the Level 2 provider.

How does it work?
The full code is available from PhonepayPlus. However, key elements to be aware of are:

- "That premium rate services comply with the law."

Clearly you cannot offer anything via a premium rate service that is illegal.

---

[38] **Source:** www.phonepayplus.org.uk/For-business/codeandhelp.aspx

- "That consumers of premium rate services are fully and clearly informed of all information likely to influence the decision to purchase, including the cost, before any purchase is made."

It is important the consumer is clearly informed of the costs.

- "That consumers of premium rate services are treated fairly and equitably."

The Code caps the amount of money a consumer can spend:

All sexual entertainment services: must terminate immediately when a maximum of £25.54 plus VAT per call has been spent.

Services aimed at, or which are particularly attractive to children, must terminate immediately when a maximum of £2.56 plus VAT per call is spent. For a subscription service, it must terminate when a maximum of £2.56 plus VAT per month has been spent.

Virtual chat services: as soon as is reasonably possible after the user has spent £8.52 plus VAT, (and every subsequent spend of £8.52 plus VAT of spend), you must:

- inform the user separately from the service or any promotion that £8.52 plus VAT has been spent; and

- terminate the service promptly if the user does not interact further with it.

For all subscription services: once a month, or every time a user has spent £17.04 plus VAT, the following information must be sent free to subscribers:

- the name of the service;
- confirmation that the service is subscription-based;
- what the billing period is (e.g. per day, per week or per month) or, if there is no applicable billing period, the frequency of messages being sent;
- the charges for the service and how they will or can arise;
- how to leave the service; and
- Level 2 provider contact details.

Chapter 8: UK Code of Broadcast Advertising (BCAP)

As with the CAP Code, the BCAP is designed to ensure marketing communications are legal, decent, honest and truthful. Most importantly for marketers, the Code is enforced in the spirit as well as the letter. In other words, it is a not a defence to say "but the Code doesn't specifically stop me" if your communication breaks the spirit of the Code.

The rules are enforced by the ASA (Advertising Standards Authority) as is the CAP Code (see Chapter 2).

The rules are similar to the CAP code. To avoid confusion, I have repeating the CAP wording in this chapter where it is relevant. BCAP exclusive items are marked with *BCAP*.

Does it affect me?
The BCAP Code applies to advertisements and programme sponsorship credits on radio and television services licensed by Ofcom. Advertisements include:

- teleshopping
- content on self-promotional TV channels
- television text
- interactive TV advertisements

BCAP Children
The protection of young viewers and listeners is always a priority. Children should be considered for all advertisements that:

1. are targeted at children or likely to be of interest to them
2. feature children whether as professionals or amateurs
3. could harmfully influence children even if not of direct interest to them

For example, advertisements for alcoholic drinks cannot use any personality who has a particular appeal to the under 18s.

8.1 General rules – BCAP Code Sections 01 and 02

1) Advertisements should not mislead, or cause serious or widespread offence or harm, especially to children or the vulnerable.

2) Marketers should deal fairly with consumers.

3) Marketing communications must comply with the law and not encourage anyone to break it.

4) Marketing communications must be easily identifiable as a marketing communication. *BCAP* The audience should quickly recognise the message as an advertisement, not a programme. As a result, you must be careful of using 'news flash' and you may not use a newsreader in your advertisement.

5) *BCAP* The responsibility for complying with the BCAP rests with the broadcasters, not the advertisers. Copy clearance, content and scheduling are the responsibility of each broadcaster.

All broadcast advertisements must be cleared before broadcast. Clearcast is the main agency for clearing advertisements and their service is free for most advertisements.

"Our copy clearance team consider over 33,000 scripts and view over 61,000 commercials every year (2012)".[39]

BCAP The RACC must clear "special category" radio advertisements. www.racc.co.uk

---

[39] **Source:** http://www.clearcast.co.uk/about-us.html

The 'special categories' for radio advertisements are:

- Consumer credit, investment and complex financial products and services
- Gambling products and services
- Alcohol products
- Medical and health and beauty products and treatments
- Food, nutrition and food supplements
- Slimming products, treatments and establishments
- Adult shops, stripograms, escort agencies and premium-rate sexual entertainment services
- Dating and introduction services
- Commercial services offering individual personal and consumer advice
- Environmental claims
- Matters of public controversy including matters of a political or industrial nature
- Religious organisations
- Charitable causes
- Films, DVDs, video, computer and console games that have an 18+ certificate or rating

For more information see www.racc.co.uk.

Misleading claims – BCAP Code Section 03
Advertisements must not be likely to mislead. You can include puffery 'exaggerated claims' that the average consumer is unlikely to take literally, provided you are not deliberately misleading.

You must include the name of the advertiser. The commercial intent must be made clear, if that is not obvious from the context.

ASDA Toy Sale

January 2011
A TV ad, for ASDA Stores Ltd (ASDA), showed a range of toys next to a banner that stated "1/2 PRICE TOYS". The voiceover said "The only serious thing in ASDA's Toy Event are the prices! Everything is at least half price! This doll's house is loads of fun. This guitar and amp, now £60. And this Toy Story Ride On, half price at £15. Pick up some great savings in our biggest toy event this year. ASDA. Saving you money every day." On-screen text throughout most of the ad stated "Majority of Stores. Subject to Availability. Furniture with Doll's House sold separately."

ASDA Stores Ltd (ASDA) said that they did not think the average consumer would believe that that applied to every toy in their stores.

The ASA ruled that the overall impression of the ad was that the toys featured were only a selection of the toys included in the "Toy Event" sale, and that, in conjunction with the claims "Everything is at least half price!" and "our biggest toy event this year", it was likely that viewers would infer that all toys were included in the sale. They concluded that, in the absence of a qualifying statement, the ad was misleading.

If you are quoting prices in your communications, you must include material information which is:

- the main characteristics of the product;
- the identity (for example, a trading name) and geographical address of the marketer and any other trader on whose behalf the marketer is acting;
- the price of the advertised product, including taxes, or if the price cannot be calculated in advance, how the price will be calculated;
- delivery charges;

- the arrangements for payment, delivery, performance or complaint handling. You only have to explain these if your arrangements are not what a consumer would normally expect; and
- whether consumers have the right to withdraw or cancel.

Forbidden practices
BCAP It is forbidden to use images of very brief duration, or any other technique that is likely to influence consumers, without their being fully aware of what has been done.

8.2 Making advertising clear – BCAP Code Section 03
Advertisements must be clearly distinguishable from editorial and programme content.

You cannot claim that a product will help the consumer win in a game of chance or a lottery.

You cannot claim that your livelihood will be in jeopardy if the consumer does not buy the product.

You may not promote a pyramid promotion scheme (sometimes called Ponzi schemes) where consumers pay for the opportunity to receive payments primarily from other new members, not the sale or consumption of products.

8.3 Pricing – BCAP Code Section 03
Essentially, if you quote a price, it must be the price the consumer must pay. This includes any non-optional duties, fees and taxes, plus any delivery charges. If any of these costs are variable, then you must explain how the costs are calculated.

If prices are shown VAT-free, then the VAT rates that some consumers will have to pay must be prominently stated.

For example, "business price £X, excl VAT at 20%", or you can show two prices, one for business customers and one for the public.[40]
If the price of one product depends on buying another one (such as "buy product x, get product y half price"), then it must be clear what the consumer must pay or do to get the advertised price.

BCAP An additional BCAP requirement is that, if the product can be purchased by instalments, the total price of the product/service, the frequency of the instalments as well as the instalment price must be quoted in equal prominence.

'Free/gratis/without charge'
'Free' means free! Do not describe something as free and then make the consumer pay. You must be clear what the consumer has to do to get the free offer.

A product is not 'free':

- if the consumer has to pay other charges to get it – such as postage, packaging, handling or administration costs
- where the consumer has to buy a product to get another one free:
    - you cannot increase the price of the product that has to be bought to cover the cost of the promotion
    - you cannot reduce the quality of the product that the consumer must buy

'Free trial' must not be used to describe "satisfaction or your money back" offers, because the consumer has to pay for the product to try it.

---

[40] **Source:** http://www.cap.org.uk/News-Reports/Media-centre/2013/Two-pricing-rule-changes.aspx

CAP and BCAP give examples of using the word 'free'[41]:

✓ "free wallchart when you buy Thursday's paper" is justified if the paper is sold without a wallchart on other days for the same price;

✓ "25% extra free", for a bottle of shampoo, is justified if the bottle contains 25% more shampoo than is usually supplied at that price;

✓ "free travel insurance for customers who book their holiday online" is justified if customers who book the same journey by telephone are offered the same price but not offered free insurance or if internet customers who choose to buy their insurance from a different provider pay the same for their holiday as those who choose to take advantage of the marketer's insurance offer;

✓ "free delivery for customers who spend over £50 on groceries" is justified if the retailer does not offer free delivery when the grocery spend is less than £50.

In each case, the company can demonstrate that there is a genuinely separate element that is 'free'. If the customer does not comply with the rules of the offer, they do not receive the free addition.

Slightly more confusing is the use of the word 'free' in part of a package of products. For example, if a mobile phone subscription offers a certain amount of airtime, texts and voicemail, this is described as a package. Customers cannot choose to have only part of this package, so the marketer cannot claim that it is 'free'.

If a new element is introduced, such as picture texts, at no additional cost, then the marketer may claim this is 'free' but only for a short time (usually up to 6 months). After 6 months, the customer will assume this is part of the package, and no longer a free benefit.

---

[41] **Source:** Guidance Note: Guidance on the use of the "free", published by CAP (Sept 2010)

Introductory offers: existing products to potential new customers:[42]

Similar rules apply to using 'free':

✓ 'Free sports bag for new members' of a gym would be justified if the sports bag was offered to all new members, who could choose whether or not to take it, and new members paid the same price whether or not they took the bag.

✓ 'Free calls for the first three months' could be justified, even on an ongoing basis where the paid-for item is a package. You would need to show that the offer was open only to new customers and that existing customers who paid the same price did not receive inclusive calls but received an otherwise identical service: you would have demonstrated that the calls were more than was usually supplied for the price and so justified the use of 'free'.

New product

As the product is new, the marketer cannot show that there has been a product at the same price before. To justify the use of 'free', the marketer must show that the customer has a genuine choice over whether to have the free item or not. For example, if a new magazine is launched with the offer 'Free binder with issue one' with a genuine choice of whether the customer took the binder, the marketer would have shown that the offer was a conditional-purchase promotion and justified the use of 'free'.

8.4 Availability – BCAP Code Section 03

If you advertise a product, it must be available.

BCAP Broadcasters must be satisfied that advertisers have made a reasonable estimate of demand.

If demand is likely to exceed supply, you must be clear that this is a limited offer.

---

[42] **Source:** Guidance Note: Guidance on the use of the "free", published by CAP (Sept 2010)

If the offer is just testing the amount of potential demand, you must state this clearly.

Any restrictions on availability must be clear, such as geographic or age restrictions.

BCAP Broadcasters must be satisfied that advertisers will not refuse to take an order for the product, or refuse to deliver it in a reasonable time frame, in an attempt to sell another one (a technique known as 'switch selling').

You cannot mislead the consumer about the possibility of finding a product elsewhere to encourage the consumer to buy the product on less favourable conditions.

8.5 Comparisons – BCAP Code Section 03
Claims that your product is superior ('superlative claims') will be assumed to be against all competing products. Claims that your product is superior must be supported by evidence – the only time you do not need to have evidence is if your claims are 'puffery' that is something the consumer is unlikely to take literally. If you claim your product is superior, you must be clear exactly what is superior.

Comparison with an identifiable competitor: the general advice is, be very careful here. You must compare products that are intended for the same purpose, you must make claims that are clear, relevant and verifiable. You must not cause confusion with the competitor.

EU agricultural products and foods: if these have a 'designation of origin' then you must compare only with other products with the same designation.

Price comparisons: the rule is to compare like with like. If you are comparing your price against your competitors, it must be for the same product, or at least a product for the same need.

For example, you can compare the price of your non-branded baked beans with a competitor's price for premium branded baked beans. You must make the basis of their comparison clear.

8.6 Endorsements and testimonials – BCAP Code Section 03

Put simply, keep a record and be clear what the testimonial is about – if it is for Product X, do not claim it is for something different.

If you quote an endorsement or testimonial, you must be able to show that it is genuine and keep a copy of it. You must also get permission to use it. You do not need permission to make an accurate quote from a published source, test, trial, professional endorsement, research facility or professional journal.

Endorsements that are obviously fictitious may be used in communications.

Never use Royal Arms or Emblems or Royal Warrant without prior permission. Never imply you are endorsed by the ASA or BCAP!

8.7 Guarantee/Warranty/After-sales service/Care packages – BCAP Code Section 03

If you offer a guarantee, you must abide by it. Be very clear about any restrictions. *BCAP* The broadcaster must be satisfied that the advertiser will supply the full terms of the guarantee before the consumer is committed.

BCAP The broadcaster must be satisfied that, if the consumer claims a refund under the guarantee, the advertiser will refund promptly.

If you are offering products in European Economic Area (EEA) states, be careful about the amount and language of the after-sales service. If you cannot offer after sales service in the same EEA State as the customer or if the service will be in a different language from that of the EEA State, then be clear about this. *BCAP* The broadcaster must be satisfied that the advertiser will explain this to the consumer before the contract is concluded.

EEA States are:

Austria	Greece	Netherlands
Belgium	Hungary	Norway
Bulgaria	Iceland	Poland
Cyprus	Ireland	Portugal
Czech Republic	Italy	Romania
Denmark	Latvia	Slovakia
Estonia	Liechtenstein	Slovenia
Finland	Lithuania	Spain
France	Luxembourg	Sweden
Germany	Malta	United Kingdom

8.8 Offence – *BCAP* - BCAP Code Section 04

"Advertisements must not be harmful or offensive. Advertisements must take account of generally accepted standards to minimise the risk of causing harm or serious or widespread offence. The context in which an advertisement is likely to be broadcast must be taken into account to avoid unsuitable scheduling."

BCAP The BCAP rules are wider than the CAP rules.

Harm

Advertisements must contain nothing that could cause physical, mental, moral or social harm to persons under the age of 18.

Advertisements must not exploit the special trust that persons under the age of 18 place in parents, guardians, teachers or other persons.

Advertisements must not include material that is likely to condone or encourage behaviour that prejudices health or safety.

Radio only – Advertisements must not include sounds that are likely to create a safety hazard, for example, to those listening to the radio while driving.

Television only – Advertisements must not include visual effects or techniques that are likely to affect adversely members of the audience with photosensitive epilepsy.

Television only – Advertisements must not be excessively noisy or strident.

Offence

Advertisements must not cause serious or widespread offence against generally accepted moral, social or cultural standards.

Advertisements must not condone or encourage harmful discriminatory behaviour or treatment. Advertisements must not prejudice respect for human dignity.

Advertisements must not condone or encourage violence, crime, disorder or anti-social behaviour.

Advertisements must not distress the audience without justifiable reason. Advertisements must not exploit the audience's fears or superstitions.

Television only – Animals must not be harmed or distressed as a result of the production of an advertisement.

Advertisements must not condone or encourage behaviour grossly prejudicial to the protection of the environment.

Quooker UK Ltd

March 2013
A TV ad, for a boiling water tap, showed a woman using the tap for a variety of kitchen tasks such as filling a cafetiere, preparing pasta for cooking and blanching vegetables. A voice-over described what she was doing in each scene. At one point the woman was shown filling a see-through bowl containing several teats from babies' bottles while the voice-over stated "sterilise baby bottles in a flash".

The ASA considered that the claim "sterilise baby bottles in a flash" combined with the image of the tap being run, implied that sterilisation would occur instantly. They considered that impression was reinforced because the woman was shown filling a bowl, rather than the saucepans used in some other scenes, which suggested that no more boiling needed to take place.

The ASA ruled the ad broke BCAP Code rules 1.2 (Social responsibility), 4.1 and 4.4 (Harm and offence) because the ad implied that babies' bottles could be sterilised instantly on contact with boiling water when that was not the case. The ASA concluded that the ad was irresponsible and could lead to harm.

8.9 Children – BCAP Code Section 05
The BCAP code is tougher on advertising to children than the CAP Code. Not only is the content of the advertisement important, but also the context and scheduling of the advert.

"The context in which an advertisement is likely to be broadcast and the likely age of the audience must be taken into account to avoid unsuitable scheduling. Advertisements that are suitable for older children and young persons but could distress younger children must be sensitively scheduled or placed."

BCAP Children must be protected from advertisements that could cause physical, mental or moral harm.

BCAP Advertisements that are suitable for older children but could distress younger children must be sensitively scheduled (see scheduling section below).

BCAP Advertisements must not:

- condone, encourage or unreasonably feature behaviour that could be dangerous for children to copy
- implicitly or explicitly discredit established safety guidelines
- condone, encourage or feature children going off alone or with strangers
- condone or encourage practices that are detrimental to children's health
- condone or encourage bullying
- portray or represent children in a sexual way

Advertisements may however inform children about dangers or risks associated with potentially harmful behaviour.

Peer pressure
Children tend to want to be part of the in-crowd and marketers must not exploit this. You cannot exploit children's credulity, loyalty, vulnerability or lack of experience.

Specifically, you cannot make children feel inferior or unpopular if they do not buy the advertised product, nor can you make them feel that they are being uncourageous, undutiful or disloyal if they do not buy the product.

Under new guidance on using children in peer-to-peer marketing, you cannot make a child feel unpopular, inferior, disloyal, uncourageous or undutiful if the child does not participate in peer-to-peer marketing (encouraging friends to buy the product).[43]

Children cannot commit to buy complex or costly products without adult permission.

You may not exaggerate what an ordinary child can attain by using the product.

You may not exploit children's susceptibility to charitable appeals. For charity-linked promotions, you must explain the extent that their participation will help the charity.

BCAP An advertisement for a children's product or service must not use qualifiers such as 'only' or 'just' to make the price seem less expensive.

BCAP TV advertisements for a toy, game or similar children's product costing over £30, must state the actual or approximate price.

Direct exhortation
You must not directly exhort children to buy or to persuade an adult to buy a product for them. You cannot ask a child to buy something in order to enter a promotion. You cannot target a direct response mechanism to buy a product at children.

Promotion
The rules are not very different from the rules of sales promotions to adults: promotions must include a prominent closing date, if applicable, and must not exaggerate the value of a prize or the chances of winning it. *BCAP* The main difference is that you must make clear if adult permission is required. *BCAP* If advertisement is for a competition, then the skill required must be in line with the age of the child.

---

43 **Source:** http://www.cap.org.uk/News-Reports/Media-centre/2012

Distance selling
You cannot target a direct response mechanism to buy a product at children.

Checklist for marketing to children[44]

Do:
- Be sensitive to their age, vulnerability and lack of experience
- Tell them to get adult approval if the product is pricey or complex
- Make it easy to judge size, characteristics and performance of a product
- Include the price if the product costs £30 or more

Don't:
- Make a direct appeal to children to buy advertised products
- Ask them to persuade their parents (or other adults) to buy on their behalf, this is 'pester-power'
- Undermine parental authority (for example "using this is more important than tidying your room")
- Show, encourage or cause any dangerous or immoral behaviour
- Imply children will be unpopular or disloyal if they do not buy the product or peer-to-peer market the product
- *BCAP* Use ambiguous language such as 'just' and 'only', when you include a price
- Advertise age-inappropriate products (for example, alcohol or gambling)
- Invite the child to enter a sales promotion if there is a cost

If you are planning to market to children, use CHECK, the Children's Ethical Communications Kit. It contains rules, legislation and guidance about marketing and communicating to children. CHECK is an Advertising Association initiative, in partnership with Turner Media Innovations and is developed with the help of the entire advertising industry. Go to http://www.check.uk.com.

---

[44] **Source:** http://www.check.uk.com/sales-promotions.html partially adapted

Scheduling advertisements[45]

You cannot advertise certain products in between, or near, programmes that appeal to young people. The restrictions are based on whether products are age appropriate.

Under-18s:

- alcoholic drinks
- most gambling
- betting tipsters
- slimming products
- religious matter
- live premium-rate services

Under-16s:

- (TV only) food or drink products that are high in fat, salt or sugar (HFSS)
- lotteries
- football pools
- equal-chance gaming
- prize gaming
- some gaming machines
- medicines, vitamins or other dietary supplements
- computer games carrying an 18+, 16+ or 15+ rating
- matches
- trailers for films or videos carrying an 18-certificate or 15-certificate

Under-10s:

- sanitary protection products
- condoms

---

[45] **Source:** BCAP section 32 scheduling http://www.check.uk.com/scheduling-restrictions.html

> **MTV Networks Europe**
>
> **January 2013**
> A TV ad for the MTV series The Valleys featured young people at a house party. Scenes included a woman bouncing on the sofa so you could see her pants, a man flexing his pecs, a women flexing her breasts in a low cut top, two women kissing, men and women kissing and a woman pulling up a man's top and touching his stomach.
>
> The voice-over said, "The harder they party, the harder they fall. Will they make it in Cardiff, or will they just end up back in the valleys? Brand new reality, coming soon to MTV".
>
> The ASA ruled that the ad did not contain any explicit nudity, but did include a number of shots that focused on breasts and a number of suggestive scenes such as a woman moving her hand down a man's torso, and two women being photographed on a mobile phone while kissing. Many of the interactions between individuals at the party were depicted with a sexual element and the overall tone of the ad was sexual. The ad was not suitable for broadcast when younger children might be watching and that the ad was not suitable for broadcast before 7.30pm.

Advertisements that might frighten or distress young children or are otherwise unsuitable for them must have careful scheduling to minimise the risk of children hearing them. Radio broadcasters are expected to consider whether advertisements are scheduled during school runs and school holidays. There are no specific 'time bars' and no 'watershed' for radio advertisements. There are scheduling times for TV advertisements.

Advertising food to children
Generally advertisements must not disparage good dietary practice and must avoid anything likely to encourage poor nutritional habits or an unhealthy lifestyle, especially in children – on TV, radio and in non-broadcast ads.

Radio food advertisements (except those for fresh fruit or fresh vegetables) targeted at pre-school or primary school children must not include licensed characters or celebrities popular with children.

Note that any brand characters (puppets, persons or characters) that the advertiser has created may be used to sell the products they were designed to sell. So, for example, in a radio advertisement, you could not use Thomas the Tank Engine to sell a breakfast cereal but Kellogg's may use Tony the Tiger.

BCAP For TV advertisements, restrictions only apply to High Fat, Salt and Sugar (HFSS) foods. You cannot target television advertising or sponsorship of HFSS products towards children. Television adverts and sponsorship for HFSS food cannot be shown around programmes made for children, or of particular appeal to children.

Swizzels Matlow Ltd

August 2012
A website for a confectionery manufacturer, www.swizzels-matlow.com, featured a virtual area called "Swizzels Town", in which a user could navigate between various locations representing different products. The areas included games, photographs and videos.

A game on the cola bottle section of Swizzels Town stated, "COLA CAPERS. Cheeky children visiting the factory have scattered Cola Bottles all around the corridors - you must rush round and collect them all while avoiding the angry parents. Collect all the Cola Bottles to move onto the next room in the factory. There are 3 rooms. Good Luck!" Over three levels the game's character could collect almost one hundred cola bottle sweets. If the character was caught by the 'angry parents' they would lose a life.

The ASA ruled that the game, which was relatively long in duration, was aimed at young children and condoned eating a large number of sweets whilst hiding this fact from one's parents. They concluded that the Cola Capers game irresponsibly encouraged poor nutritional habits and an unhealthy lifestyle in children.

8.10 *BCAP* Privacy – BCAP Code Section 08
The CAP code states that "Individuals should be protected from unwarranted infringements of privacy.". However, the BCAP code specifically mentioned 'living individuals':

"Living individuals should be protected from unwarranted infringements of privacy. Broadcasters should respect an individual's right to his or her private and family life, home and correspondence. Advertisements featuring an individual should not imply that that individual endorses a product if he or she does not."

The rules are different for radio and for TV advertisements.

TV: On the whole, living people should not appear or be referred to without their permission. If they appear as part of a crowd scene, this is acceptable.

Radio: You can refer to living people without their permission provided they are not shown in an offensive, adverse or defamatory way. However, it is good practice to gain their permission.

You must not interfere with an individual's private or family lives.

Impersonations and soundalikes are allowed where listeners can recognise them as impersonations and where the person(s) concerned would have no reason to object. Again, it is good practice to seek advance permission.

If you are referring to well-known fictional characters, the copyright holder must give permission.

8.11 Political advertisements – BCAP Code Section 07

The Communications Act 2003 and BCAP Code ban political advertising. The term 'political' is used in the Code in a wider sense than 'party political'. The prohibition includes, for example, campaigning for the purposes of influencing legislation. Ofcom, not the ASA, decides if an advertisement is political.

8.12 Other BCAP rules for specialised areas

These specialised areas are beyond the scope of this Handbook. There are rules on the marketing of:

- medicines, medical devices, treatments and health
- weight control and slimming
- food, food supplements
- financial products
- faith, religion
- charities
- gambling
- lotteries
- alcohol
- motoring
- betting tipsters
- introduction and dating services
- private investigation agencies

If these apply to you, please check the relevant areas of the BCAP code. Go to http://www.cap.org.uk/Advertising-Codes/Broadcast-HTML.aspx.

Further Reading

Government advice
Set up by the government, this gives simple, clear explanations for a range of business issues in plain English. It claims to be "simpler, clearer, faster" and actually is! Thoroughly recommended for checking up on legislation. Go to: https://www.gov.uk/browse/business

Trading Standards websites
Trading Standards in local areas of the UK have their own websites. A good source of accessible and clear information about aspects of trading regulations.

ERWIN (Everything Regulation, Whenever It's Needed)
This is a one-stop web site for all Trading Standards, Environmental Health, Licensing and Fire Safety business related information across England and Wales. It is designed to provide regulatory services information in an innovative way that will make it more accessible and useful for businesses. Go to: http://www.everythingregulation.org.uk

Ardi Kolah Guru in a Bottle – Essential Law for Marketers
Ardi Kolah is a lawyer who understands marketing. His latest edition in the 'Guru in a Bottle' series is a comprehensive review of marketing law for marketers: Essential Law for Marketers (2013) published by Kogan Page

CAP Copy Advice Team
Free of charge advice on advertisements. The team will look at ideas, concepts, imagery and copy for your advertisements and claim to offer fast and confidential advice. Go to: http://www.cap.org.uk/Advice-Training-on-the-rules/Bespoke-Copy-Advice.aspx

CHECK, the Children's Ethical Communications Kit
Contains rules, legislation and guidance about marketing and communicating to children. Check is an Advertising Association initiative, in partnership with Turner Media Innovations and is developed with the help of the entire advertising industry. Go to http://www.check.uk.com.

Index

Advertising, 16, 17, 18, 19, 21, 22, 23, 25, 26, 38, 41, 42, 51, 55, 59, 68, 77, 79, 80, 82, 85, 89, 97, 100, 102, 103, 105

B2B, 12, 16, 21, 48, 68

B2C, 12, 16, 48, 68

brand, 14, 18, 41, 103

Broadcast, 22, 24, 47, 54, 59, 80, 85, 86, 95, 97

competition, 73, 99

competitors, 16, 30, 31, 35, 93

Cookie, 65, 68, 77, 78, 79

costs, 29, 31, 41, 49, 53, 64, 83, 89, 90, 100

direct mail, 22, 66, 71, 76

Direct marketing, 22, 67, 76

e-commerce, 48, 73

email, 48, 50, 59, 68, 69, 71, 72, 73, 80

endorsement, 35, 94

GE, 33, 35, 48, 63, 92, 94

international, 46, 55

internet, 32, 44, 47, 48, 51, 91

logo, 14, 55, 56

loyalty, 39, 80, 98

media, 25, 31, 38, 39, 41, 42, 77, 100

opt-in/opt-out, 71, 72, 75, 77, 80

packaging, 16, 17, 25, 31, 54, 90

partnerships, 68, 73

planning, 42, 76, 100

price, 14, 19, 25, 28, 29, 30, 31, 32, 33, 35, 41, 42, 43, 45, 49, 51, 53, 60, 63, 64, 88, 89, 90, 91, 92, 93, 94, 99, 100

Product, 12, 13, 14, 16, 17, 18, 26, 28, 29, 30, 31, 32, 33, 34, 35, 36, 39, 40, 41, 42, 43, 44, 45, 51, 53, 54, 55, 56, 57, 72, 88, 89, 90, 92, 93, 94, 98, 99, 100, 104

radio, 55, 85, 86, 87, 95, 102, 103, 104, 105

Sales, 13, 18, 22, 25, 35, 40, 42, 43, 48, 73, 94, 99, 100

Sales promotion, 22, 40, 42, 43, 99, 100

service, 12, 14, 16, 25, 28, 33, 35, 48, 54, 58, 59, 60, 61, 63, 64, 72, 73, 75, 76, 78, 81, 82, 83, 84, 86, 90, 92, 94, 99

Services, 16, 24, 46, 47, 48, 49, 50, 53, 58, 59, 61, 62, 63, 64, 75, 78, 79, 81, 82, 83, 84, 85, 87, 101, 106

sponsorship, 85, 103

television, 55, 85, 96, 103

Twitter, 23, 26

value, 40, 99

website, 23, 25, 51, 52, 58, 60, 62, 63, 68, 78, 79

Cambridge Marketing Handbooks

This Legal Handbook is one in a series of Handbooks for marketing practitioners and students, designed to cover the full spectrum of the Marketing Mix. The other Handbooks include:

- Distribution
- Product
- Communications
- Services
- Philosophy
- Research
- Stakeholder
- Pricing Points
- Digital